JUVENILE CRIME

OPPOSING VIEWPOINTS®

Andrea C. Nakaya, *Book Editor*

Bruce Glassman, *Vice President*
Bonnie Szumski, *Publisher*
Helen Cothran, *Managing Editor*

OPPOSING
VIEWPOINTS®
SERIES

GREENHAVEN PRESS
An imprint of Thomson Gale, a part of The Thomson Corporation

THOMSON

GALE

Detroit • New York • San Francisco • San Diego • New Haven, Conn.
Waterville, Maine • London • Munich

For more information, contact
Greenhaven Press
27500 Drake Rd.
Farmington Hills, MI 48331-3535
Or you can visit our Internet site at http://www.gale.com

Cover credit: © Banan Stock

LIBRARY OF CONGRESS CATALOGING-IN-PUBLICATION DATA

Juvenile crime : opposing viewpoints / Andrea C. Nakaya, book editor.
   p. cm. — (Opposing viewpoints series)
Includes bibliographical references and index.
  ISBN 0-7377-2945-7 (lib. : alk. paper) — ISBN 0-7377-2946-5 (pbk. : alk. paper)
   1. Juvenile delinquency—United States. 2. Juvenile delinquency—United
States—Prevention. 3. Juvenile justice, administration of—United States.
I. Nakaya, Andrea C., 1976– . II. Opposing viewpoints series (Unnumbered)
HV9104.J834 2005
364.36'0973—dc22   2005040320

Printed in the United States of America

> "Congress shall make no law...abridging the freedom of speech, or of the press."

First Amendment to the U.S. Constitution

The basic foundation of our democracy is the First Amendment guarantee of freedom of expression. The Opposing Viewpoints Series is dedicated to the concept of this basic freedom and the idea that it is more important to practice it than to enshrine it.

Contents

Chapter 4: How Can the U.S. Juvenile Justice System Be Improved?

Why Consider Opposing Viewpoints?

"The only way in which a human being can make some approach to knowing the whole of a subject is by hearing what can be said about it by persons of every variety of opinion and studying all modes in which it can be looked at by every character of mind. No wise man ever acquired his wisdom in any mode but this."

John Stuart Mill

In our media-intensive culture it is not difficult to find differing opinions. Thousands of newspapers and magazines and dozens of radio and television talk shows resound with differing points of view. The difficulty lies in deciding which opinion to agree with and which "experts" seem the most credible. The more inundated we become with differing opinions and claims, the more essential it is to hone critical reading and thinking skills to evaluate these ideas. Opposing Viewpoints books address this problem directly by presenting stimulating debates that can be used to enhance and teach these skills. The varied opinions contained in each book examine many different aspects of a single issue. While examining these conveniently edited opposing views, readers can develop critical thinking skills such as the ability to compare and contrast authors' credibility, facts, argumentation styles, use of persuasive techniques, and other stylistic tools. In short, the Opposing Viewpoints Series is an ideal way to attain the higher-level thinking and reading skills so essential in a culture of diverse and contradictory opinions.

In addition to providing a tool for critical thinking, Opposing Viewpoints books challenge readers to question their own strongly held opinions and assumptions. Most people form their opinions on the basis of upbringing, peer pressure, and personal, cultural, or professional bias. By reading carefully balanced opposing views, readers must directly confront new ideas as well as the opinions of those with whom they disagree. This is not to simplistically argue that everyone who reads opposing views will—or should—change his or her opinion. Instead, the series enhances readers' understanding of their own views by encouraging confrontation with opposing ideas. Careful examination of others' views can lead to the readers' understanding of the logical inconsistencies in their own opinions, perspective on why they hold an opinion, and the consideration of the possibility that their opinion requires further evaluation.

Evaluating Other Opinions

To ensure that this type of examination occurs, Opposing Viewpoints books present all types of opinions. Prominent spokespeople on different sides of each issue as well as well-known professionals from many disciplines challenge the reader. An additional goal of the series is to provide a forum for other, less known, or even unpopular viewpoints. The opinion of an ordinary person who has had to make the decision to cut off life support from a terminally ill relative, for example, may be just as valuable and provide just as much insight as a medical ethicist's professional opinion. The editors have two additional purposes in including these less known views. One, the editors encourage readers to respect others' opinions—even when not enhanced by professional credibility. It is only by reading or listening to and objectively evaluating others' ideas that one can determine whether they are worthy of consideration. Two, the inclusion of such viewpoints encourages the important critical thinking skill of objectively evaluating an author's credentials and bias. This evaluation will illuminate an author's reasons for taking a particular stance on an issue and will aid in readers' evaluation of the author's ideas.

It is our hope that these books will give readers a deeper understanding of the issues debated and an appreciation of the complexity of even seemingly simple issues when good and honest people disagree. This awareness is particularly important in a democratic society such as ours in which people enter into public debate to determine the common good. Those with whom one disagrees should not be regarded as enemies but rather as people whose views deserve careful examination and may shed light on one's own.

Thomas Jefferson once said that "difference of opinion leads to inquiry, and inquiry to truth." Jefferson, a broadly educated man, argued that "if a nation expects to be ignorant and free . . . it expects what never was and never will be." As individuals and as a nation, it is imperative that we consider the opinions of others and examine them with skill and discernment. The Opposing Viewpoints Series is intended to help readers achieve this goal.

David L. Bender and Bruno Leone,
Founders

Greenhaven Press anthologies primarily consist of previously published material taken from a variety of sources, including periodicals, books, scholarly journals, newspapers, government documents, and position papers from private and public organizations. These original sources are often edited for length and to ensure their accessibility for a young adult audience. The anthology editors also change the original titles of these works in order to clearly present the main thesis of each viewpoint and to explicitly indicate the opinion presented in the viewpoint. These alterations are made in consideration of both the reading and comprehension levels of a young adult audience. Every effort is made to ensure that Greenhaven Press accurately reflects the original intent of the authors included in this anthology.

Introduction

*"Juveniles murder almost ten people every day. That's
nearly a quarter of all murders committed."*
—*American Medical Association*

*"No more than 1 in every 360 persons ages 10–17 was
arrested for a Violent Crime . . . in 2002, or about one-
third of 1% of all the juveniles ages 10–17 living in the
U.S."*
—*Office of Juvenile Justice and Delinquency Prevention*

Beginning in the late 1980s there was a substantial increase in
juvenile crime in the United States. According to the Federal
Bureau of Investigation, the number of juveniles arrested for
violent crimes grew by nearly 65 percent between 1987 and
1995. In 1996 news editor Steve Macko commented, "It now
seems that every day we are hearing about horrendous violent crimes being committed by juveniles." Statistics show
that youth were indeed committing an increasing number of
criminal acts. News of these crimes appeared with increasing
frequency in the media; disturbing headlines, such as "6-
Year-Old Boy Charged with Attempted Murder of Baby" and
"Thirteen-Year-Old Convicted of First-Degree Murder"
evoked disbelief and fear. Years later, in 2005, headlines such
as these continue to appear, but, according to official statistics, juvenile crime has decreased substantially in the United
States. Despite these statistics, though, there is widespread
debate over the extent of the juvenile crime problem. Some
people believe it is no longer a serious problem. Others contend that juvenile crime in the United States has actually become more common and more violent.

Nationwide crime statistics show a wave of juvenile crime
that began in the late 1980s, reached a peak in the mid-1990s,
and then began to decrease significantly. Writer Stephen
Chapman discusses this change: "In the late 1980s and early
'90s, kids went on a violent binge, boosting their murder rates
by half." He adds, "Many experts looked toward the future

and assured us that things were about to get even worse. . . . The Council on Crime in America predicted a 'coming storm of juvenile violence.'" However, as Chapman explains, dire predictions such as this did not turn out to be true. In fact, he says, "If you turned those predictions upside down, you'd get a pretty good picture of what has happened in reality." According to Jeffrey Butts, director of the Program on Youth Justice, juvenile crime is now lower than it has been in a long time. "By 2002," he says, "violent juvenile crime had dropped nationwide to levels not seen in more than a decade. On a per capita basis, the rate of violent crime arrests in 2002 was lower than at any time since 1973." Statistics from the Office of Juvenile Justice and Delinquency Prevention (OJJDP) data also show this trend. According to the OJJDP, the juvenile arrest rate for murder fell 72 percent between 1993 and 2002.

Many people point to these statistics as evidence that juvenile crime is no longer a serious threat to Americans. They believe that while juvenile crime does occur, the extent of the problem is far less than suggested by the media. Gallup poll statistics show that American adults hold a vastly inflated view of the amount of crime committed by juveniles; according to a 2000 poll, Americans believed juveniles to be responsible for 43 percent of all violent crime in the United States when in fact, according to OJJDP data, they were responsible for only 12 percent. Author Mike Males blames these false beliefs on the media. "In scare campaigns against adolescents, the news media not only uncritically repeat official claims," says Males, "they actively embellish them with sinister cover stories and apocalyptic tales of suburban mayhem. The message is screamed from headlines, magazine covers and network specials: Adolescents are 'wild in the streets'; teens everywhere are 'killer kids.'" Critics such as Males claim that juvenile crime does not pose a grave threat to the safety of Americans. Steven Chapman asserts that "by 2003, Americans were as safe, or safer, from the threat of violent juvenile crime than they had been any time in the past three decades."

However, other people point out that official crime statistics may not tell the full story. Many believe that while the numbers may show a decrease, juvenile crime is still prevalent, and more violent than ever before. That is the conclusion of the 2001 report *Youth Violence: A Report of the Surgeon General*, which found that while arrest rates have deceased, youth violence has not. According to the report, the fact that youth are not being arrested as often as they were a decade ago does not mean that youth violence has decreased. "As weapons carrying declined, so too did arrest rates, perhaps because the violence was less injurious or lethal," found researchers, "but the amount of underlying violent behavior . . . did not change much—if anything, it appears to have increased." The report concludes, "The magnitude of serious violence occurring beneath the police radar should warn us that youth violence is a persistent problem demanding a focus on prevention." In a 2002 report, by the Josephson Institute of Ethics, researchers warned that "many people think youth violence is declining. . . . But actually it remains as widespread as ever." According to the institute's researchers, "The ferocity of violence has waned, but the amount has not."

With limited budgets and resources for combating crime, communities must make choices about what types of crimes they should focus on. Thus, citizens and government officials continue to debate the extent of juvenile crime. Many other facets of this controversial topic also inspire extensive public debate. The authors in *Opposing Viewpoints: Juvenile Crime* offer opinions on some of these topics in the following chapters: What Are the Causes of Juvenile Crime and Violence? How Should the Criminal Justice System Treat Juvenile Offenders? How Can Juvenile Crime and Violence Be Prevented? and How Can the U.S. Juvenile Justice System Be Improved? Central to the discussions in all of these chapters is the prevalence of juvenile crime.

CHAPTER 1

What Are the Causes of Juvenile Crime and Violence?

Chapter Preface

On April 20, 1999, Columbine High School students Eric Harris, eighteen, and Dylan Klebold, seventeen, opened fire on students and teachers in their suburban Denver, Colorado, school. Entering the school in full-length black coats that concealed their weapons, the two teenagers went on an hour-long rampage, at the end of which they had killed fifteen people, including themselves, and wounded twenty-three others. While there have been numerous school shootings before and after that day, this was America's deadliest. As people struggled to understand what had caused this tragedy, many pointed to the ease with which the shooters had obtained their weapons: a semiautomatic handgun, a rifle, and two shotguns. In the debate over the causes of juvenile crime and violence, many experts focus on the role that guns play in criminal behavior.

Many opponents of gun ownership argue that in the United States a major cause of school shootings is the availability of guns to youth. As journalist Bob Levin points out, "You can't shoot people without a gun." He believes that because it is so easy for youth to obtain guns, firearms become a common, and deadly, way for children to express their anger. "Once their rage is stoked and justified," says Levin, "once they're deep into the darkness and set to let loose as kids have long done in fast cars or on bad drugs or simply with a clothesline in a closet, they can simply grab a handy semiautomatic and . . . go blow away their classmates." The Consumer Federation of America echoes Levin's belief that school shootings would be far less likely if America instituted tougher gun-control laws. According to the Federation, "School shootings are preventable, if parents would take guns out of their homes and if Congress would regulate America's out-of-control gun industry. . . . Research reveals that school shootings often involve guns from the shooter's home, or that of a relative."

However, other people, such as San Diego deputy district attorney Michael Carlton, believe that gun access is not the real problem. According to Carlton, "The bottom line is, I personally believe that there are more than enough adequate laws to punish people and that the solutions to this type of violence are not through the passage of additional laws related to weapons." Instead, he argues, the real issue that needs to be addressed is why youth are angry enough to look for a gun in the first place. Timothy Wheeler, a proponent of gun ownership, agrees. "Blaming anything or anyone but the perpetrator himself has become the order of the day," he says, but "what law can remedy fatal character defects? By banning the culture of guns and hunting we will not stop teen murderers. But by rebuilding a culture of loving, moral guidance for our children we will."

Youth violence occurs frequently in the United States and around the world, sparking debate over the underlying causes of criminal juvenile behavior. The authors in the following chapter offer various perspectives on this issue.

"The romanticized . . . visions of violence our children are being bombarded with by the media [have] become part of a toxic mix turning some of them into killers."

The Media Contribute to Youth Violence

Part I: Joe Lieberman; Part II: Jeff McIntyre

In the following two-part viewpoint, the authors maintain that the media should be held responsible for increasing incidences of violence and crime among youth. In Part I Joe Lieberman argues that the media aggressively and deceptively market violent products to children, products that have been proven in hundreds of studies to greatly increase the risk of violent behavior. In Part II Jeff McIntyre maintains that the media have an extremely powerful influence over youth, and that children quickly learn to imitate the violent behavior they have seen portrayed in the media. Lieberman is a U.S. senator representing Connecticut. In 2000 he was the Democratic candidate for vice president. McIntyre is the legislative and federal affairs officer for the American Psychological Association's Public Policy Office, a national organization that advises congressional decision makers on a wide variety of issues.

As you read, consider the following questions:
1. How has the entertainment industry been deceptive, according to Lieberman?
2. In McIntyre's opinion, what does excellent children's programming show about the media's effects?

Part I: Joe Lieberman, testimony before the U.S. Senate Commerce Committee, Washington, DC, September 13, 2000. Part II: Jeff McIntyre, statement before the U.S. Senate Subcommittee on Telecommunication and the Internet, Committee on House Energy and Commerce, Washington, DC, September 13, 2004.

I

We are here today [September 13, 2000] to talk about the threat of violence to our country, and in particular the troubling way that the entertainment media are promoting and selling adult-rated products to our children. But we are also talking on a broader level about the thread of values that connects us as a nation, and the growing concern about the impact the popular culture is having on our moral fabric. That connection is critical to understanding what's at stake here, and I want to take a few moments to discuss it.

Deteriorating Values

As you know . . . this conversation has been reverberating around the country for the last several years. There is widespread anxiety that our common values are deteriorating, that our standards of decency and civility and safety are eroding, that our families are weakening, and, as a result, that our quality of life is suffering. Many of us in public office . . . have tried to give voice to these concerns, in particular to the complaints of parents who feel locked in a losing competition with the culture to raise their children.

Then came Columbine,[1] a psychic breaking point for so many of the American people. It was a warning that the culture of carnage surrounding our children may have gone too far, and that the romanticized and sanitized visions of violence our children are being bombarded with by the media had become part of a toxic mix turning some of them into killers. So we pleaded with the leaders of the entertainment industry to join us at the table . . . and work with us to reduce the risk of another student rampage and help us fight the larger problem of youth violence.

The Media Are at Fault

The report released by the FTC [Federal Trade Commission] this week indicates just how far we still have to go. Rather than helping to shoulder some of the growing burden

---

1. In April 1999 two students at Columbine High School in Littleton, Colorado, shot and killed twelve students and one teacher, and injured twenty-three others. The boys then shot themselves.

on parents, according to the FTC, the entertainment industry too often has chosen to go behind their back, targeting the sale of violent, adult-rated products directly to children. In fact, the FTC found dozens of internal marketing plans which show conclusively that the movie, music, and video game industries were purposely cutting out the middle mom and dad and routinely, aggressively, and intentionally marketing these violent, harmful products to young audiences.

This practice is deceptive, it is outrageous, and it must stop. The leaders of these industries have to realize that they cannot tell parents that these products are inappropriate for their kids and then turn around and market them to their kids. That makes a mockery of the ratings systems that parents depend on to make the right decisions for their children. It greatly decreases the effectiveness of these warnings. And it greatly increases the odds that children will be exposed to materials that hundreds of studies have conclusively shown can be harmful to them. . . .

What we are asking for today is not censorship, but simply better citizenship, especially from these major entertainment companies that shape our culture. These same companies contribute so much to our culture, our economy, and to the American experience. They make so many wonderful products that entertain, educate, and elevate us as a people. But they are also contributing to some serious national troubles, and we need their cooperation if we are to make things better.

II

I have conducted years of work related to children and the media as a negotiator for the development of a television ratings system, as an advisor to the Federal Communications Commission's V-Chip[2] Task Force, as a member of an informal White House Task Force on Navigating the New Media, as a member of the steering committee for the Decade of Behavior Conference on Digital Childhood, and most importantly, as a representative of the research and concerns of the over 150,000 members and affiliates of the American

---

2. The V-chip allows television receivers to block specific programs based on the programs' content.

Psychological Association. I also have an appointment on the Oversight Monitoring Board for the current television ratings system.

Media Violence Causes Youth Violence

At the heart of the issue of children and the media is a matter long addressed by psychological research—the effects of repeated exposure of children to violence. The media violence issue made its official debut on Capitol Hill [Washington, D.C.] in 1952 with the first of a series of congressional hearings. That particular hearing was held in the House of Representatives before the Commerce Committee. The following year, in 1953, the first major Senate hearing was held before the Senate Subcommittee on Juvenile Delinquency, who convened a panel to inquire into the impact of television violence on juvenile delinquency.

Gamble. © 1996 by *The Florida Times-Union*. Reproduced by permission of Ed Gamble.

There have been many hearings since the 1950's, but there has been only limited change—until recently. Media violence reduction is fraught with legal complications. Nevertheless, our knowledge base has improved over time, with the publication of significant and landmark reviews. Based on these research findings, several concerns emerge when violent material is aggressively marketed to children.

Foremost, the conclusions drawn on the basis of over 30 years of research contributed by American Psychological Association (APA) members—including the Surgeon General's report in 1972, the National Institute of Mental Health's report in 1982, and the industry funded, three-year National Television Violence Study in the 1990's—show that the repeated exposure to violence in the mass media places children at risk for: increases in aggression; desensitization to acts of violence; and unrealistic increases in fear of becoming a victim of violence, which results in the development of other negative characteristics, such as mistrust of others.

A Psychological Fact

If this sounds familiar, it is because this is the foundation upon which representatives of the public health community—comprised of the American Psychological Association, the American Academy of Pediatrics, and the American Medical Association—issued a joint consensus statement in 2000 on what we absolutely know to be true regarding children's exposure to violence in the media.

Certain psychological facts remain well established in this debate. As APA member Dr. Rowell Huesmann stated before the Senate Commerce Committee, just as every cigarette you smoke increases the chances that someday you will get cancer, every exposure to violence increases the chances that, some day, a child will behave more violently than they otherwise would.

Hundreds of studies have confirmed that exposing our children to a steady diet of violence in the media makes our children more violence prone. The psychological processes here are not mysterious. Children learn by observing others. Mass media and the advertising world provide a very attractive window for these observations.

The excellent children's programming (such as *Sesame Street*) and pro-social marketing (such as that around bicycle helmets) that exists is to be commended and supported. Psychological research shows that what is responsible for the effectiveness of good children's programming and pro-social marketing is that children learn from their media environment. If kids can learn positive behaviors via this medium, they can learn the harmful ones as well.

Ratings Systems

The role of ratings systems in this discussion merits attention. There continues to be concern over the ambiguity and implementation of current ratings systems. It appears that ratings systems are undermined by the marketing efforts of the very groups responsible for their implementation and effectiveness. That . . . displays a significant lack of accountability and should be considered when proposals for industry self-regulation are discussed.

Also undermined here are parents and American families. As the industry has shown a lack of accountability in the implementation of the existing ratings system, parents have struggled to manage their family's media diet against misleading and contradictory information. (For instance, marketing an R rated film to children under 17.) While the industry has made some information regarding the ratings available, more information regarding content needs to be made more accessible, more often. As with nutritional information, the content labeling should be available on the product and not hidden in distant websites or in the occasional pamphlet.

Generally speaking, most adults see advertising as a relatively harmless annoyance. However, advertising directed at children, especially at young children, that features violence generates concern. The average child is exposed to approximately 20,000 commercials per year. This is only for television and does not include print or the Internet. Much of this is during weekend morning or weekday afternoon programming. Most of the concern stems not from the sheer number of commercial appeals but from the inability of some children to appreciate and defend against the persuasive intent of marketing, especially advertising featuring violent product.

Children Must Be Protected

A recent Federal Trade Commission report on the Marketing of Violence to Children heightens these concerns. As a result of the "Children's On-Line Privacy Protection Act" the Federal Trade Commission has ruled that parents have a right to protect their children's privacy from the unwanted solicitation of their children's personal information. We would argue that, based on the years of psychological research on violence prevention and clinical practice in violence intervention, parents also have the right to protect their children from material that puts them at risk of harm. With the considerations in place for children's privacy, the precedent for concern about children's health and safety is well established.

Decades of psychological research bear witness to the potential harmful effects on our children and our nation if these practices continue.

> *"Banning specific media images will have little or no impact on the problem of youth crime."*

The Media Should Not Be Blamed for Youth Violence

Henry Jenkins

In the following viewpoint Henry Jenkins argues that media content may give violent youth a way to express their rage, but it does not cause that rage. Media images do not have universal meanings, he maintains; instead they are interpreted by youth in different ways, depending on their different personalities and life experiences. In his opinion, some youth already have the desire to commit violence, a desire that comes from the way they have been treated by others, not from exposure to media violence. He believes the media cannot be blamed when these youth misinterpret certain images and use them as an inspiration for violence. Jenkins is director of the Comparative Media Studies Program and a professor of literature at the Massachusetts Institute of Technology.

As you read, consider the following questions:

1. According to the author, how do people define their own media environment?
2. How can criminal actions result after reading the Bible, according to Jenkins?
3. In Jenkins's opinion, what did the Littleton case suggest about the most powerful influences on children?

Henry Jenkins, testimony before the U.S. Senate Commerce Committee, Washington, DC, May 4, 1999.

The shootings at Columbine High School in Littleton, Colorado several weeks ago[1] have justly sparked a period of national soul searching. This incident was shocking and tragic; it seems to defy any rational understanding. As parents, educators, citizens, political leaders, we demand to know how such a thing could have happened and we desperately want to believe we can come up with policies or laws that can prevent it from happening again. We want ANSWERS. But we are only going to come up with valid answers if we start by asking the right sets of QUESTIONS. So far, most of the conversation about Littleton has reflected a desire to understand what the media are doing to our children. Instead, we should be focusing our attention on understanding what our children are doing with media.

No Clear Connection Between Media and Youth Violence

As more information becomes available to us, it is becoming increasingly clear that Eric Harris and Dylan Klebold, the two Littleton shooters, had an especially complex relationship to popular culture. Various pundits have pointed their fingers at video games, violent movies, television series, popular music, comic books, websites, youth subcultures, and fashion choices to locate the cause of their violent behavior. What have we learned so far? Harris and Klebold played video games. Not surprising—roughly 80 percent of American boys play video games. Harris and Klebold spent a great deal of time online. According to [author] Don Tapscott's *Growing Up Digital: The Rise of the Net Generation*, 11 percent of the world's computer users are under the age of 15. Thirty-six percent of American teens use an online service at home, 49 percent at school, and 69 percent have been online at least once in their lifetime, compared to 40% of the total population that has been online. They engaged in online gaming. According to [author] Jon Katz, estimates of online gamers in the United States alone run as high as 15 to 20 million people. Harris and Klebold watched a range of films, in-

---

1. In April 1999 two students at this high school shot and killed twelve students and one teacher, and injured twenty-three others. The boys then shot themselves.

cluding *The Matrix*, which has been the top money earner in four of the last five weeks. They listened to various popular music groups, some relatively obscure (kmfdm), some highly successful (Marilyn Manson). They may have borrowed certain iconography from the Goth subculture, a subculture that has a history going back to the 1980s and which has rarely been associated with violence or criminal activity. They may have worn black trench coats. None of these cultural choices, taken individually or as an aggregate, differentiates Harris and Klebold from a sizable number of American teenagers who also consumed these same forms of popular culture but have not gone out and gunned down their classmates. The tangled relationship between these various forms of popular culture makes it impossible for us to determine a single cause for their actions. Culture doesn't work that way.

Media Consumption Is Complex

Cultural artifacts are not simple chemical agents like carcinogens that produce predictable results upon those who consume them. They are complex bundles of often contradictory meanings that can yield an enormous range of different responses from the people who consume them.

Like the rest of us, Harris and Klebold inhabited a hypermediated culture. The range of media options available to us has expanded at a dramatic rate over the past several decades. We see this expansion everywhere—the introduction of CDs led to an expansion of the range of popular music kept in circulation; the introduction of cable television has dramatically increased the spectrum of television programs we can watch; the introduction of digital media introduces us to a much broader array of ideas and stories that we would have encountered in a world of centralized gatekeepers; niche marketing has led to an explosion of new specialized magazines, many of them targeting youth. New media technologies are being introduced at an astonishing rate enabling a more participatory relationship to media culture. In such a world, each of us make choices about what kinds of media we want to consume, what kinds of culture are meaningful or emotionally rewarding to us. None of us devote our attention exclusively to only one program, only one recording star, only one network, or only one medium. People define their own media environment through their own particular choices from the huge menu of cultural artifacts and channels of communication that surround us all the time. Some teens are drawn towards the angst-ridden lyrics of industrial music; others are happily jitterbugging to neo-swing. Selling popular culture to our kids isn't quite the same thing as selling cigarettes to our kids. When it comes to popular culture, we all "roll our own." We cobble together a personal mythology of symbols, images, and stories that we have adopted from the raw materials given us by the mass media, and we invest in those symbols and stories meanings that are personal to us or that reflect our shared experiences as part of one or another subcultural community. In the case of Harris and Klebold, they drew into their world the darkest, most alienated, most brutal images available to them and they turned those images into the vehicle of their personal demons, their antisocial impulses, their psychological maladjustment, their desire to hurt those who have hurt them.

In this case, those choices and investments had lethal results.

Symbols

Banning black trench coats or violent video games doesn't get us anywhere. The black trench coats or the song lyrics are only symbols. To be effective in changing the nature of contemporary youth culture, what we want to get at are the meanings that are associated with those symbols, the kinds of affiliations they express, and more importantly, the feelings of profound alienation and powerlessness that pushed these particular kids (and others like them) over the edge. Consuming popular culture didn't make these boys into killers; rather, the ways they consumed popular culture reflected their drive towards destruction. For most kids most of the time, these forms of popular culture provide a normal, if sometimes angst ridden, release of frustration and tension. Sometimes, indeed most often, as the old joke goes, a cigar is only a cigar and a black trench coat is only a raincoat.

Symbols don't necessarily have fixed or universal meanings. Symbols gain meanings through their use and circulation across a variety of contexts. Some of those meanings are shared, some of them are deeply personal and private, but once we perceive a need to express a particular feeling or idea, human beings are pretty resourceful at locating a symbol that suits their needs.

A History of Concern

Americans have been concerned about the prevalence of violence in the media and its potential harm to children and adolescents for at least 40 years. The body of research on television violence has grown tremendously since the first major Federal reports on the subject in 1972 and 1982 (National Institute of Mental Health, 1982; U.S. Surgeon General's Scientific Advisory Committee on Television and Social Behavior, 1972). During this period, new media emerged—video games, cable television, music videos, and the Internet. As they gained popularity, these media, along with television, prompted public concern and research attention.

Youth Violence: A Report of the Surgeon General, 2001.

It is relatively easy to get rid of one or another symbol. Some symbols—the swastika for example—maintain power over thousands of years, although they have often radically shifted meaning over that time. But most of the time, symbols have a very limited shelf life. Half the time media activists focus their energies on combating examples of popular culture that have little or no commercial appeal to begin with. Computer games such as *Custer's Revenge*, *Death Trap*, or *Postal*, which have been the center of so much debate about video game violence had only limited commercial success and are far from the bread and butter of the video game industry, which is, for the most part, far more dependent on its sports-focused games than on combat games. The images found in such marginal works are certainly outrageous, but they are so outrageous that they attract few customers; they alienate their potential market and collapse of their own accord. It is much harder to get rid of the feelings that those symbols express.

Using the Media to Express What Is Within

I don't need to remind you how many violent crimes have been inspired by one or another passage from the *Bible*. When we hear such stories about religious fanatics committing violent crimes, we recognize that reading the *Bible* did not cause these murders, even though some of the violent images that got stuck in the killers' minds originated in one or another passage of scripture. When we encounter such situations, we say that these criminal actions resulted from a misreading of the *Bible*, that they took those images out of context, that the killers invested those passages with their own sickness. The same claim can be made about the works of popular culture. Popular films and television programs may not have the spiritual depth of the *Bible*, they will almost certainly not survive as long, but they are still complex works that express many different ideas and lend themselves to many different uses and interpretations. Sometimes one or another image from mass culture does become part of the fantasy universe of a psychotic, does seem to inspire some of their antisocial behavior, but we need to recognize that these images have also been taken out of context, that they have been ascribed with idiosyncratic meanings. Despite the mass size of the audience for some of the cultural products we are discussing, there are tremendous differences in the way various audience members respond to their influence.

Shortly after I learned about the Columbine High School shootings, I received e-mail from a 16-year-old web mistress who had written to thank me about some comments I made in an interview on media fandom. She gave me the URL for her website and what I found there was truly inspirational. She had produced an enormous array of poems and short stories drawing on characters from one or another popular television series, film, or comic book series. She had organized her friends—both in her local community and elsewhere in the country—to write their own stories and poems. Most of them showed a careful crafting and an expressive quality that most high school composition teachers would love to foster in their students. She had made her own selections from the range of popular culture aimed at American youth. For example, she was especially drawn towards more realistic stories dealing with the social relations between teens, to such television series as *My So-Called Life*, *Dawson's Creek*, *Beverly Hills 90210*, and *Party of Five*, but she was also drawn towards some series that have Gothic overtones, such as *Buffy the Vampire Slayer* or Neil Gaiman's *The Sandman* comic books. She reached into contemporary youth culture and found there images that emphasized the power of friendship, the importance of community, the wonder of first romance. She used the web to create a space where she and other teens could share what they had created with each other. The mass media didn't make Harris and Klebold violent and destructive any more than it made this girl creative and sociable. These teens drew on the stories that circulate within popular culture as resources for expressing things that were within them. These teens used media as a tool for communicating their perceptions of the world. Their websites look very different because they are very different teens. Even when they are using some of the same images, they don't mean the same things to them. . . .

Direct Experiences Are the Most Powerful

Popular culture is only one influence on our children's fantasy lives. As the Littleton case suggests, the most powerful influences on children are those they experience directly, that are part of their immediate environment at school or at home. In the case of Harris and Klebold, these influences apparently included a series of social rejections and humiliations and a perception that adult authorities weren't going to step in and provide them with protection from the abuse directed against them from the "in crowd."

We can turn off a television program or shut down a video game if we find what it is showing us is ugly, hurtful, or displeasing. We can't shut out the people in our immediate environment quite so easily. Many teenagers find going to school a brutalizing experience of being required to return day after day to a place where they are ridiculed and taunted and sometimes physically abused by their classmates and where school administrators are slow to respond to their distress and can offer them few strategies for making the abuse stop. Media images may have given Harris and Klebold symbols to express their rage and frustration, but the media did not create the rage or generate their alienation. What sparked the violence was not something they saw on the internet or on television,

29

not some song lyric or some sequence from a movie, but things that really happened to them. . . .

Some of the experts who have stepped forward in the wake of the Littleton shootings have accused mass media of teaching our children how to perform violence—as if such a direct transferral of knowledge were possible. The metaphor of media as a teacher is a compelling but ultimately misleading one. As a teacher, I would love to be able to decide exactly what I want my students to know and transmit that information to them with sufficient skill and precision that every student in the room learned exactly what I wanted, no more and no less. But, as teachers across the country can tell you, teaching doesn't work that way. Each student pays attention to some parts of the lesson and ignores or forgets others. Each has their own motivations for learning. Whatever "instruction" occurs in the media environment is even more unpredictable. Entertainers don't typically see themselves as teaching lessons. They don't carefully plan a curriculum. They don't try to clear away other distractions. Consumers don't sit down in front of their television screens to learn a lesson. Their attention is even more fragmented; their goals in taking away information from the media are even more personal; they aren't really going to be tested on what they learn. Those are all key differences from the use of video games as a tool of military training and the use of video games for recreation. The military uses the games as part of a specific curriculum with clearly defined goals, in a context where students actively want to learn and have a clear need for the information and skills being transmitted, and there are clear consequences for not mastering those skills. None of this applies to playing these same or similar games in a domestic or arcade context. . . .

Banning Specific Images Will Not Work

Banning specific media images will have little or no impact on the problem of youth crime, because doing so gets at symbols, not at the meanings those symbols carry and at the social reality that gives such urgency to teens' investments in those cultural materials. . . . What we need to do is learn more than we have so far about what children are doing with these new media, what place the contents of popular culture have assumed in their social and cultural life, and what personal and subcultural meanings they invest in such symbols. . . .

We all want to do something about the children at risk. We all want to do something about the proliferation of violent imagery in our culture. We all want to do something to make sure events like the Littleton shootings do not occur again. But repression of youth culture is doomed not only to fail but to backfire against us.

> "*Confounding factors should not distract us from the overwhelming evidence linking single parents or absent parents to the propensity [of juveniles] to commit crimes.*"

Single Parenthood Increases the Risk of Juvenile Crime

Jennifer Roback Morse

In the following viewpoint Jennifer Roback Morse argues that children who grow up with only one parent are at an increased risk of becoming juvenile criminals. Because these children frequently receive less adult supervision and may not form strong human attachments during infancy, they may not develop empathy and self-control, explains Morse. In consequence, they are less likely to be deterred from criminal activity. Morse is a research fellow at the Hoover Institution at Stanford University and author of *Love and Economics: Why the Laissez-Faire Family Doesn't Work.*

As you read, consider the following questions:

1. What relationship did Chris Couglin and Samuel Vuchinich find between stepparent or single-parent households and delinquency?
2. How does the author respond to anecdotes about thriving children of single parents?
3. Why is a posture of neutrality among family arrangements wrong, in Morse's opinion?

Jennifer Roback Morse, "Parents or Prisons," *Policy Review*, August/September 2003, p. 49. Copyright © 2003 by The Hoover Institution. Reproduced by permission.

The basic self-control and reciprocity that a free society takes for granted do not develop automatically. Conscience development takes place in childhood. Children need to develop empathy so they will care whether they hurt someone or whether they treat others fairly. They need to develop self-control so they can follow through on these impulses and do the right thing even if it might benefit them to do otherwise.

All this development takes place inside the family. Children attach to the rest of the human race through their first relationships with their parents. They learn reciprocity, trust, and empathy from these primal relationships. Disrupting those foundational relations has a major negative impact on children as well as on the people around them. In particular, children of single parents—or completely absent parents—are more likely to commit crimes.

Without two parents, working together as a team, the child has more difficulty learning the combination of empathy, reciprocity, fairness, and self-command that people ordinarily take for granted. If the child does not learn this at home, society will have to manage his behavior in some other way. He may have to be rehabilitated, incarcerated, or otherwise restrained. In this case, prisons will substitute for parents.

The observation that there are problems for children growing up in a disrupted family may seem to be old news. The public has become more aware that single motherhood is not generally glamorous in the way it is sometimes portrayed on television. [Author] David Blankenhorn's *Fatherless America* depicted a country that is fragmenting along family lines. Blankenhorn argued, and continues to argue in his work at the Institution for American Values, that the primary determinant of a person's life chances is whether he grew up in a household with his own father. . . .

It has become increasingly clear that the choice to become a single parent is not strictly a private choice. The decision to become an unmarried mother or the decision to disrupt an existing family does not meet the economist's definition of "private." These choices regarding family structure have significant spillover effects on other people. We can no longer deny that such admittedly very personal decisions have an impact on people other than the individuals who choose.

There are two parts to my tale. The first concerns the impact of being raised in a single-parent household on the children. The second involves the impact that those children have on the rest of society.

Current Events

The two parts of my story were juxtaposed dramatically on the local page of the *San Diego Union-Tribune* one Wednesday morning at the end of January [2003]. "Dangling Foot Was Tip-Off," explained the headline. A security guard caught two teenaged boys attempting to dump their "trash" into the dumpster of the gated community he was responsible for guarding. The guard noticed what looked like a human foot dangling out of the bag. He told the boys he wanted to see what was in it. They refused. As a private security guard, he had no authority to arrest or detain the pair. He took their license plate number and a description of the duo and called authorities.

The "trash" proved to be the dismembered body of the boys' mother. They had strangled her, chopped off her head and hands, and ultimately dumped her body in a ravine in Orange County. The boys were half-brothers. The elder was 20 years old. His father had committed suicide when the boy was an infant. The younger boy was 15. His father had abandoned their mother.

At first glance, the second news item seems unrelated to the first. On the same page of the newspaper, a headline read, "Mayor Wants 20% Budget Cuts." This particular mayor presides over the city of Oceanside [California], the same city where the brothers tried to dump their mother's body. In nearby Vista, the mayor's "State of the City Address Warns of Possible Deep Cuts." In Carlsbad, one freeway exit to the south, the city's finances were "Called Good Now, Vulnerable in Future." All these mayors were tightening their cities' belts in response to severe budget cuts proposed by [former] California Governor Gray Davis. The governor expects to reduce virtually every budget category in the state budget except one: the Department of Corrections.

Therein lies the tale: These stories are connected by more

than just the date and time of their reportage. The increase in serious crimes by younger and younger offenders is absorbing a greater percentage of state resources, necessarily crowding out other services. [These cases] do have something to do with the budget woes of state and local governments.

Impact of Having a Parent in Jail

It's now estimated that 10 million young people nationwide have had a mother or father—or both—behind bars at some point in their lives; though most come from poor, minority backgrounds, no segment of society is immune.

Their welfare isn't just their problem. "If we don't start paying attention to these children, they are going to end up being major consumers of our social services systems, and they are likely to be involved in the juvenile justice system and later on in the adult justice system as well," says criminal justice Prof. Barbara Bloom. . . . "If we focus on these kids now and provide them the kind of support they need, then we can prevent both the economic and social costs to society later on."

Carolyn Kleiner, *U.S. News & World Report*, April 29, 2002.

Several other high-profile cases of juvenile crime fit this pattern. Alex and Derek King, aged 12 and 13 respectively, bludgeoned their sleeping father to death with a baseball bat and set fire to the house to hide the evidence. The mother of the King brothers had not lived with them for the seven years prior to the crime. Derek had been in foster care for most of those years until his behavior, including a preoccupation with fire, became too difficult for his foster parents to handle. The murder took place two months after Derek was returned to his father's custody.

John Lee Malvo, the youthful assistant in the Beltway Sniper case,[1] came to the United States with his mother from Jamaica. His biological father has not seen him since 1998. His mother evidently had a relationship with John Allen Mohammed, who informally adopted her son. Mohammed himself, probably the mastermind if not the triggerman in the se-

---

1. In October 2002, ten people were killed and three critically injured by sniper attacks in the Washington, D.C., area. Seventeen-year-old Malvo and John Allen Mohammed were convicted for the shootings.

rial sniper case, was also a fatherless child. According to one of his relatives, Mohammed's mother died when he was young, his grandfather and aunt raised him because his dad was not around.

While these high-profile cases dramatize the issues at stake, excessive focus on individual cases like these can be a distraction. As more information about the [families in these cases] comes in, for instance, a variety of mitigating or confounding circumstances might emerge to suggest that factors other than living in a single-parent home accounted for the horrible crime. A family history of mental illness, perhaps, or maybe a history of child abuse by the mother toward the children may surface as contributing factors. And indeed, many of the most gruesome crimes are committed not by fatherless children in single-mother households, but by motherless boys, growing up in a father-only household. Some, such as John Lee Malvo, had essentially no household at all. But these confounding factors should not distract us from the overwhelming evidence linking single parents or absent parents to the propensity [of juveniles] to commit crimes.

The Statistical Evidence

This result has been found in numerous studies. The National Fatherhood Initiative's *Father Facts*, edited in 2002 by Wade Horn and Tom Sylvester, is the best one-stop shopping place for this kind of evidence. Of the many studies reviewed there, a representative one was reported in the *Journal of Marriage and the Family* in May 1996. Researchers Chris Couglin and Samuel Vuchinich found that being in stepparent or single-parent households more than doubled the risk of delinquency by age 14. Similarly, a massive 1993 analysis of the underclass by [researchers] M. Anne Hill and June O'Neill, published by Baruch College's Center for the Study of Business and Government, found that the likelihood that a young male will engage in criminal activity increases substantially if he is raised without a father.

These studies, like most in this area, attempted to control for other, confounding factors that might be correlated with living in a single-parent household. If single mothers have less money than married mothers, then perhaps poverty is the fundamental problem for their children. But even taking this possibility into account, the research still shows that boys who grew up outside of intact marriages were, on average, more likely than other boys to end up in jail.

Another set of studies found that the kids who are actually in the juvenile justice system disproportionately come from disrupted families. The Wisconsin Department of Health and Social Services, in a 1994 report entitled "Family Status of Delinquents in Juvenile Correctional Facilities in Wisconsin," found that only 13 percent came from families in which the biological mother and father were married to each other. By contrast, 33 percent had parents who were either divorced or separated, and 44 percent had parents who had never married. The 1987 *Survey of Youth in Custody*, published by the U.S. Bureau of Justice Statistics, found that 70 percent of youth in state reform institutions across the U.S. had grown up in single- or no-parent situations.

Causal Links

There are several plausible links between single parenthood and criminal behavior. The internal dynamic of a one-parent household is likely to be different from that of a two-parent household. Two parents can supervise the child's behavior more readily than one. Misbehavior can continue undetected and uncorrected for longer periods of time [in a single-parent household] until it becomes more severe and more difficult to manage.

Likewise, the lowered level of adult input partially accounts for the lowered educational attainments of children of single parents. Such families report parents spending less time supervising homework and children spending less time doing homework. Not surprisingly, kids in these families have inferior grades and drop out of school more frequently. Leaving school increases the likelihood of a young person becoming involved in criminal behavior. It is similarly no surprise that adolescents who are left home alone to supervise themselves after school find more opportunities to get into trouble. Finally, the percentage of single-parent families in a neighborhood is one of the strongest predictors of the neighborhood's crime rate. In fact, [researchers] Wayne Osgood and Jeff Chambers, in their 2000 article in the journal *Criminology*, find that father absence is more significant than poverty in predicting the crime rate.

These kinds of factors are easy enough to understand. A more subtle connection between the fractured family and criminal behavior is the possibility that the child does not form strong human attachments during infancy. A child obviously cannot attach to an absent parent. If the one remaining parent is overwhelmed or exhausted or preoccupied, the child may not form a proper attachment even to that parent. Full-fledged attachment disorder is often found among children who have spent a substantial fraction of their infancy in institutions or in foster care. (Think of Derek King.)

An attachment-disordered child is the truly dangerous sociopath, the child who doesn't care what anyone thinks, who does whatever he can get away with. Mothers and babies ordinarily build their attachments by being together. When the mother responds to the baby's needs, the baby can relax into her care. The baby learns to trust. He learns that human contact is the great good that ensures his continued existence. He learns to care about other people. He comes to care where his mother is and how she responds to him. Eventually, he will care what his mother thinks of him.

This process lays the groundwork for the development of the conscience; caring what she thinks of him allows him to internalize her standards of good conduct. As he gets older, bigger, and stronger, his mother can set limits on his behavior without physically picking him up and carrying him out of trouble. Mother's raised eyebrow from across the room can be a genuine deterrent against misbehavior. As he matures, she doesn't even need to be present. He simply remembers what she wants him to do. Ultimately, he doesn't explicitly think about his parents' instructions. Without even considering punishments or approval, his internal voice reminds him, "We don't do that sort of thing." He has a conscience. . . .

Statistics and Probabilities

Some might respond that they personally are acquainted with many wonderful children of single parents. The parents are loving and giving; the children are thriving. But these anecdotal cases are not decisive. For every such story, we could produce a counter-story of a struggling single-parent family that fits the more distressing profile. The mother is a lovely person who did her best, but the boy got out of hand in his teenage years. Or the mother started out as a lovely person but she became preoccupied with her new boyfriend or her job troubles. Her parents are heartbroken because they can see that their grandchildren are headed for trouble.

Besides, it is important to understand what statistical evidence does and does not prove. To say that a child of a single mother is twice as likely to commit a crime as the child of married parents is not to say that each and every child of every unwed mother will commit crimes or that no child of married parents will ever commit crimes. It is simply to say that growing up with unmarried parents is a significant risk factor. . . .

What to Do?

For years we have heard that single parenthood is an alternative lifestyle choice that doesn't affect anyone but the person who chooses it. We have been instructed that society should loosen the stigma against it in order to promote individual freedom of choice. We have been scolded for being insufficiently sensitive to the plight of single mothers if we utter any criticism of their decisions. At the urging of various activist groups, the government and society at large have been developing a posture of neutrality among family arrangements. There are no better or worse forms of family, we are told. There are no "broken families," only "different families."

The premise behind this official posture of neutrality is false. The decision to become a single parent or to disrupt an existing family does affect people outside the immediate household. These words may seem harsh to adults who have already made crucial life decisions, but it is time to be candid. We need to create a vocabulary for lovingly, but firmly and without apology, telling young people what we know. Surely, telling the truth is no infringement on anyone's liberty. Young people need to have accurate information about the choices they face. For their own sake—and for ours.

"Poor quality child care multiplies the risk that children will grow up to be a threat to every American family."

Inadequate Child Care Increases the Risk of Juvenile Crime

Sanford Newman et al.

A large number of young children do not receive quality child care, report Sanford Newman, T. Berry Brazelton, Edward Zigler, Lawrence W. Sherman, William Bratton, Jerry Sanders, and William Christeson in the following viewpoint. The authors assert that chilren who receive inadequate child care are significantly more likely to become juvenile criminals. According to the authors, numerous studies show that children who do not receive good quality child care are also more likely to become poor parents themselves, increasing the risk that their own children will commit crimes. Newman is president of Fight Crime: Invest in Kids, an organization dedicated to reducing crime; Brazelton is a professor at Harvard Medical School; Zigler is a professor at Yale University; Sherman is a professor at the University of Pennsylvania; Bratton is former police commisioner of New York City; Sanders is former San Diego chief of police; and Christeson is research director of Fight Crime: Invest in Kids.

As you read, consider the following questions:
1. According to the authors, what did nearly nine out of ten police chiefs say would greatly reduce crime?
2. Why do children frequently receive poor child care, in the authors' opinion?

Sanford Newman, T. Berry Brazelton, Edward Zigler, Lawrence W. Sherman, William Bratton, Jerry Sanders, and William Christeson, "America's Child Care Crisis: A Crime Prevention Tragedy," Fight Crime: Invest in Kids, January 2000. Copyright © 2000 by Fight Crime: Invest In Kids, Washington, DC. Reproduced by permission.

Fight Crime: Invest in Kids is a national anti-crime organization led by hundreds of those on the front lines of the battle against crime and violence: police chiefs, sheriffs, police organization leaders, prosecutors, crime victims and those from whom murder has taken loved ones.

Our members are determined to put dangerous criminals behind bars. But we also know that no punishment after someone gets hurt can undo the agony crime leaves in its wake. When children don't get the right start in life, all of us are endangered. Good school readiness child care is one of our most powerful weapons against crime, while poor quality child care multiplies the risk that children will grow up to be a threat to every American family. Yet millions of eligible children are missing out on the help they need to get that right start in life.

In a recent [1999] survey conducted by George Mason University professors Stephen Mastrofski and Scott Keeter, nearly nine of ten police chiefs said America could greatly reduce crime by expanding educational child care programs and after-school programs. Nine out of ten said that if America doesn't boost investments in child care programs now, it will pay far more later in crime, welfare, and other costs.

When police chiefs were asked to rate various strategies "on their value as a crime prevention tool," educational child care was given the highest rating for effectiveness by three to ten times more chiefs than such alternatives as trying more juveniles as adults, building more juvenile detention facilities, or installing more metal detectors in schools.

Just the Facts, Please

This report isn't about ideology or philosophy; it's about facts. Like other Americans, crime fighters and academic researchers hold a range of views on whether it would be desirable for more parents to leave the workforce to stay home with their children. The fact is most parents are working, and their children are in some form of child care. Their tender minds and emotions are being powerfully shaped by the quality of that care.

The issue for law enforcement is whether the care the children receive while their parents are working will be good enough to help the kids get a good start in life, or whether it will be care that damages their development and ultimately endangers the public safety. Wishful thinking won't save lives. Good educational child care will.

The time for philosophical debate about whether such investments "might work" is past. The proof is in, and the facts are clear. . . .

School Readiness Child Care

Rigorous behavioral studies, hard experience and brain research tell the same story: in the first several years of life, children's intellects and emotions are being powerfully shaped.

The kind of stimulation and interaction the child receives—touching, holding, rocking, talking, showing—determines the permanent development of the brain. While learning continues throughout life, this brain development proceeds at an astounding pace in the first several years.

Recent brain research is confirmed by years of behavioral research comparing children who had good nutrition, stimulation, and nurturing when they were babies with others not so lucky. These nurturing factors have a substantial impact on brain function at age twelve, and an even greater impact by age fifteen.

The child care programs which have proven most effective in preventing future delinquency and crime are those that supplement quality developmental day care with home visits and other efforts to coach parents in child-rearing skills. For example:

High/Scope Perry Preschool Program. In Ypsilanti, Michigan, the High/Scope Educational Research Foundation randomly divided low-income three- and four-year-olds into two groups. Half received no special services, while the others were enrolled in a quality preschool program, including a weekly home visit, until they started kindergarten. When the children reached age 27, arrest records showed that those who had received quality preschooling were only one-fifth as likely to be "chronic offenders," with more than four arrests.

In other words, those who were denied the quality preschool and parenting education visitor program as preschoolers were five times more likely to become chronic lawbreakers in adulthood!

Syracuse University Family Development Program. Researchers found that subsequent delinquency was cut dramatically when families were provided educational child care, parenting-education home visits, and other services beginning prenatally and continuing until the children began elementary school. Ten years later:

- Among those children who had not received the early childhood services, nearly one in five had already been charged with an offense. Nearly one in ten were already "chronic offenders," with more than four arrests or charges of being ungovernable. And . . . many of these offenses were serious.

- Among those children who had received the extra services, only one in twenty had even been charged with being ungovernable, and only 1.5 percent had actually been delinquent.

In other words, failing to provide these babies and toddlers with good educational child care and related services multiplied by ten times the risk that they would become delinquent as teens.

Of course, the benefits of these programs are not limited to crime prevention. When the High/Scope toddlers became adults, for example, they were far better able to support themselves and their families than those left out of the program. Among males, the children who received preschool and home visitor services were seven times more likely to earn over $24,000 a year.

While earnings were lower for females, nearly three times as many of the preschooled females as of those left out of the program (48 percent vs. 18 percent) were earning more than $12,000 a year. Those who received preschool and home visits as toddlers were also 25 percent less likely ever to have received welfare or other means-tested social services as adults.

Females who had participated in the preschool program were two and a half times more likely to earn a high school diploma (84 percent vs. 35 percent), five times more likely to be married at age 27 (40 percent vs. 8 percent) and had one-third fewer out-of-wedlock births than the control group.

But the bottom line for law enforcement is that providing these proven "right-start" services dramatically reduces the risk that children will grow up to become criminals. Failing to provide kids with these services sharply increases crime and costs lives.

Getting Results in the Real World

These results are not limited to small, model programs. For example, North Carolina's pioneering Smart Start program is spending $78 million a year on enhancing access to quality child care and other services for children under six. A new study by the University of North Carolina's Frank Porter Graham Center shows that children in the child care centers receiving substantial quality-improvement help from Smart Start were only about half as likely to have behavior problems in kindergarten.

The flip side of that statement is equally telling: Kids in centers not receiving the Smart Start services were nearly twice as likely to be disruptive in kindergarten. This is important because research consistently shows that children who exhibit problem behaviors in the early grades are at far greater risk than other children of becoming teen delinquents and adult criminals.

A nationwide study of child care confirms the point that quality matters when it comes to problem behaviors later in life. *The Children of the Cost Quality Study Go to School* research was conducted in four different states by a team from four different universities. The study first rated child care centers for quality. Years later, when the children who had been in the various centers were eight years old, their behavior was evaluated.

Children of high school–educated mothers who received good quality child care had no more behavior problems than the children of college-educated mothers. But, children of high school–educated mothers from poor quality child care had significantly more behavior problems. . . . Good quality child care levels the playing field.

If any doubt remained that a large-scale government-funded initiative could produce results similar to High/Scope's Perry Preschool, it has been erased by the new results from a long-term study of Chicago's Child-Parent Centers (CPC) that have now [in 2000] served 100,000 three- and four-year-olds in Chicago's poorest neighborhoods. Compared to the 989 children served in 20 CPCs in 1984, similar youngsters left out of the program were 70 percent more likely to have been arrested for a violent crime by age 18, 67 percent more likely to have been retained a grade in school and 85 percent more likely to have been placed in special education. The children who received the CPC program were 29 percent more likely to graduate from high school than the kids left out of the program.

Quality Child Care Prevents School Behavior Problems

At age eight, at-risk children who had been in *good* child care centers in the years before they started school had no more behavior problems than children of the best-educated mothers. But those at-risk kids who had been in *poor* quality child care centers had significantly higher behavior problems.

Problem Behaviors Score at Age 8

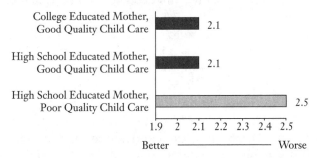

College Educated Mother, Good Quality Child Care — 2.1

High School Educated Mother, Good Quality Child Care — 2.1

High School Educated Mother, Poor Quality Child Care — 2.5

1.9 2 2.1 2.2 2.3 2.4 2.5

Better ——————— Worse

Fight Crime: Invest in Kids, 2000.

Taken as a whole, these research breakthroughs make clear that "early care and nurture have a decisive, long-lasting impact on how people develop, their ability to learn, and their capacity to regulate their own emotions." It is to our distinct advantage to put the teachings of this science to work.

Child Storage Is Not Child Care

Especially for children burdened by other disadvantages, providing poor child care rather than quality care damages their potential to become contributing adults and increases the danger that they will grow up to engage in crime.

Of course, when their parents are working, nearly all preschool children will receive some kind of care, of whatever quality. Marriott Corporation executive Donna Klein reports that every day she finds children of service workers in hotel lobbies and dangerous cleaning supply rooms, because their low-wage working parents are unable to find decent child care at an affordable price. Other parents may take their children to family day care homes in which a provider trying to make a living while keeping fees down is caring for too many babies and toddlers, or knows too little about child development to provide the nurturing and stimulation they need. As children reach school age, and sometimes even before, desperate parents may reluctantly leave them to "take care of themselves."

Recent research makes clear that "quality child care" must do far more than keep children safe from immediate physical injury. Good child care stimulates and nurtures children to maximize their healthy intellectual and emotional development.

We can no more afford to accept child care that is merely *custodial* than we could accept assigning some children to public schools that are *custodial* rather than *instructional*.

As the Committee for Economic Development, a group of business executives from major corporations, said, "All programs for children from birth to age five—whether designated as child care, early childhood education or preschool—should focus on their educational and developmental needs and take into account what children will need to succeed in school and in life.". . .

Too Many Families Cannot Afford Adequate Child Care

Today, in large part because so many parents cannot afford quality care, millions of children are in child care so inferior in quality that it not only fails to produce positive results but may actually damage their development.

In 1991, the Committee for Economic Development declared, "The lack of availability of quality child care that is developmentally appropriate, has educational value, and is affordable has created a crisis of national proportions that affects most families but hits low-income families the hardest."

Into the new millennium, that crisis has escalated.

Today [in 2000] only 23 percent of all families with children younger than age six have one parent working and one at home. One out of four children lives with only one parent, and half of all children can now expect to live an average of at least five years in a single-parent family.

Child care is expensive. In fact, a survey by the Children's Defense Fund and the National Child Care Resource and Referral Association found that: "In every state, the cost of care for an infant in an urban area center is more than the cost of public college tuition." In more than half the states, it is more than double the cost of college. The statewide average cost of care for an infant ranges from $3,692 in Mississippi to $9,509 in Minnesota. In seven states, the average cost is more than $7,500 per year. Care for a four-year-old costs less than for an infant, but the statewide averages still range from $3,380 in Mississippi to $7,839 in Alaska.

Especially at the lower end of the average range, the quality of much of the care provided is woefully inadequate. It is nearly impossible for child care centers to provide necessary staff-to-child ratios and group sizes, and pay enough to retain appropriately trained staff, without charging higher fees. . . .

With 35 percent of America's children reaching school unprepared to succeed, schools and teachers too often are overwhelmed, jeopardizing the development and education of even those children who are adequately prepared.

From a law enforcement perspective, the child care crisis is especially severe because it strikes hardest at those most vulnerable—at-risk children. When we shortchange their child care, we increase the risk they will grow up to pose a threat to the rest of us.

*"After all these years, I realize my guidance
has not been productive, and I feel helpless
in my efforts to instill positive values in my
son's heart and mind."*

Juvenile Crime Can Occur Despite Good Parenting

J.E. Keeler

In the following viewpoint J.E. Keeler argues that youth may
commit criminal acts regardless of their parents' efforts to
bring them up with good values. She presents the example of
her son, who is in jail despite her lifelong efforts to nurture
and educate him. According to Keeler, juvenile crime occurs
because youth make erroneous choices between right and
wrong, something that can occur in spite of good parenting.
Parents of juveniles should not be blamed for their acts, she
states. Keeler is the mother of a son who has spent time in
both the juvenile and the adult justice systems.

As you read, consider the following questions:

1. How is mothers' parenting often evaluated from a no-
   win perspective, as explained by Keeler?
2. Why did the author place her son as a dependent of the
   criminal justice system?
3. According to Keeler, what do some criminologists
   suggest about criminals "aging-out" of deviant
   behaviors?

J.E. Keeler, "Debunking the Myth That Mother Is to Blame for an Offender's
Behavior," *American Jails*, March/April 2004, pp. 9–11. Copyright © 2004 by the
American Jail Association. Reproduced by permission.

In our society, mothers are expected to carry the burden of child care. They have the status of full-time experts entrusted to both nurture and educate their children. This implies that mothers are responsible to impart proper societal norms and values into the hearts and minds of their children. Mothers embrace the idea that child rearing is their job, and they see themselves as primarily responsible for the well-being of their children.

Quality of Parenting Questioned

However, even though mothers accept this role, the quality of their parenting is often questioned. A deep-seated American belief is that if parents raise their children properly, they will be law-abiding citizens. In contrast, if a child does not behave appropriately, it must be the parents' fault.

Oftentimes mothers' parenting is evaluated from a no-win perspective. They are blamed if they do [parent] and blamed if they don't [parent]. Let me explain. Even when a mother takes on the responsibility of child rearing full time, a question arises: is she capable of providing proper guidance to her child? Relevant to working mothers who are with their children only part-time, a question is, aren't mothers compromising the care of their children by being employed outside the home? Thus, mothers are blamed for their children's behaviors regardless of whether they are full-time or part-time parents. Mothers are then seen as deviant and subsequently stigmatized.

I have sensed this feeling of blame, and I have felt stigmatized by correctional personnel. However, I can understand why correctional officers might feel this way. They are exposed to mothers when the mothers are most vulnerable. Most jail personnel may not be aware of what a mother has been subjected to since the birth of her child. Let me describe my personal experience at mothering and briefly describe my efforts to instill societal norms and values into my son's psyche.

Rearing a Son

My son was brought up in a two-parent household. I chose to be a full-time, stay-at-home mother dedicated to raising my children. I became concerned about my son's inability to interact with others and obey rules when he was a toddler. He would do what he wanted, regardless of parental sanctions. By the time he was in kindergarten, his teacher was sending home daily reports describing his nonconforming behaviors. This pattern continued throughout elementary school. He was sent to numerous school districts in the hope that a "new beginning" would help him.

Throughout his elementary school years, I would propose "if-then" situations hoping that he would grasp the concept of action and consequence. For example, I would say, "If you complete all your school work this week, then I will take you to a movie on Saturday." I also applied the reverse of this principle. I would say "If you disrespect your teacher today, you will not be allowed to ride your bike after school." I attempted countless combinations trying to "hit" on the magical formula that would stimulate his desire to respect rules. Unfortunately, he continued to do things his way, regardless of consequences. By the time he was in junior high school, he was not abiding by either household or school rules. He continued to resist my and educators' efforts to stimulate conformity. The amount of my mental energy expended to teach my son proper values was exhaustive. Therefore, I sought help from psychologists and psychiatrists. I hoped that they would identify the causes of his nonconformity. It was my hope that they would understand his psyche and be able to change his approach to life. However, my son resisted all efforts of help, and he continued to conduct himself in a nonconforming manner.

A Hopeless Task

At this time, I placed him as a dependent of the juvenile court system, knowing that I would lose control of the choices in my son's life. From this point forward, juvenile justice professionals would decide what he was allowed to do and where he was to live. For the next five years, countless dedicated professionals worked with him. He underwent numerous psychological and intellectual tests to identify his problem. He was also placed in numerous treatment programs where he was given one-on-one attention from the very best in their fields. Despite these efforts, my son still did what he wanted, regardless of consequences. When confronted with his non-conforming behavior, he would blame others. He would say that others provoked him to do what he did. At this time, it became evident that he did not comprehend, nor accept, responsibility for his actions.

By the time he was 17, he had quit school and was not able to maintain employment. At numerous places of employment, he would either not show up for work or he would participate in negative behaviors. These activities forced his employers to ask him either to quit or tell him he would be fired. During this period, he would drink and drive, and he committed simple assaults on a regular basis. His behavior was indicative that he did not care to abide by societal norms and values.

A Biological Theory of Crime

- The basic determinants of human behaviour are, to a considerable degree, determined by genetics.
- These basic determinants of human behaviour may be passed from one generation to the next; criminal behaviour is genetically inherited.
- Human DNA, environmental contaminants, nutrition, hormones, physical trauma (especially to the brain) and body chemistry all combine to contribute to criminal behaviour.

Saskatchewan Education, 2002. www.sasked.gov.

At this time, my extended family began to intervene with the hope that they could help my son conform. Relatives, such as brothers, a sister, aunts, uncles, and a grandmother had my son live with them in the hope that they could change his behavior. Their efforts in Connecticut and California did not persuade my son to accept assistance from others.

My son is now an adult, and for the past 13 years, he has been in and out of numerous jails throughout the United States. Unfortunately, becoming an adult neither guaranteed that he would act maturely, nor did it stimulate his desire to conform to societal rules. Instead, it meant that he would now encounter the adult criminal justice system. This also meant that I would have to interact with criminal justice personnel in order to maintain contact with my son.

Do Criminal Justice Personnel Understand?

My contact with the criminal justice system sometimes requires me to ask correctional personnel about policies and procedures guiding the disposition of my son's case. Many times, I have encountered rude and/or abrupt correctional personnel where I sense that they are annoyed with my inquiries. The situation also means that my only contact with my son will be by visiting him in a correctional facility. While visiting, I have heard correctional officers comment to others that they do not understand why a mother would visit, especially if the inmate acts in an unappreciative or an unkind manner. What some jail personnel might not understand is that, from birth, mothers are "wired" to care for their children.

After all these years, I realize my guidance has not been productive, and I feel helpless in my efforts to instill positive values in my son's heart and mind. I have exhausted all my efforts to initiate change in his psyche. I struggle daily to cope with the psychological and emotional hardships of having lost a son to criminality. His behaviors have been the greatest heartbreak in my life.

My religious conviction had taught me that we are all free moral agents with the ability to choose between right and wrong. The cliche, "you can lead a horse to water, but you cannot make it drink," is apropos. Even though I accepted the maternal role to nurture and teach my son, I was not able to instill in my son the ability to have him choose to do what is right and to conform to societal norms and values. Thus, I now accept that I cannot change my son's behavior.

Mothers Should Not Be Seen as Deviant

I also believe the scriptural dictate that if you train up a child in the way that he shall go, when he is old, he will not depart from it. The word "old" is relative. In our society, we consider a person old enough to be responsible for his or her behavior when they are 18; they are adults. Realistically, 18 years of age does not always bring conformity to norms and values instilled upon a child from birth. In addition, some criminologists suggest that some criminals will "age-out" of deviant behaviors when they reach the ages between 35 to 40 years. This thought gives me hope that my son will age-out of criminality by the time he is 40 years old.

I now know that the only thing I can give my son is love. I can let him know I care for him, regardless of his behavior. This is all I have left; it is my sole connection with my son. I continue to hope that through my love and caring he will someday want to change and conform to societal rules and expectations.

In the meantime, I will try to understand the criminal justice process relevant to my son's convictions, and I visit him whenever possible. I do not deserve to be looked upon as deviant in my role as a mother, nor do I deserve to be treated in an unkind manner by correctional personnel. It is my hope that jail personnel will treat me respectfully and give me the benefit of the doubt that I did my best in trying to instill proper societal norms and values in my son.

"There is one factor that does track reliably through the school shootings in the past few years. In virtually every instance, the teen who did the shooting had been . . . bullied."

Bullying Is the Cause of School Violence

Richard Matthews

Bullying in schools is a serious problem that is extremely harmful to some youth, contends Richard Matthews in the following viewpoint. He believes that the constant ridicule and abuse some children receive from their classmates pushes them to commit school shootings. He advocates more school programs that teach kids to respect each other. Matthews is columnist for the *Atlanta Journal-Constitution* and a member of the newspaper's editorial board.

As you read, consider the following questions:
1. In Matthews's opinion, how does the antigun lobby use school shootings to further its agenda?
2. How does the author respond to the argument that violent video games might inspire school shootings?
3. How has the nature of bullying in schools changed, according to Matthews?

Once again the nation finds itself looking at dead and wounded children in a school, and once again it asks the same question: "Why?" And once again I watch all the hand-wringing and policy game-playing and ask, "How many times can we look at clear and incontrovertible evidence and simply ignore it?"

Looking for Causes

There's a numbing repetition and regularity in the reactions to terrible events such as the shooting spree this week at a California high school.[1] First, of course, the anti-gun lobby jumps before the nearest TV camera to insist that this wouldn't happen if we just had more gun laws. Never mind that in just about every case the shooter broke existing gun laws and would have broken any new ones; there's an agenda to be pushed, and slain teenagers make excellent props.

Silly, too, is the argument about video games turning all our children into would-be murderers. When I was a child we went to the movies every Saturday and watched good guys and bad guys blaze away for the whole film, never running out of bullets until the desert floor was littered with bodies. We then went home, where rifles and pistols were far more readily available than today, and didn't shoot anybody, at school or anywhere else.

Actually, if there's any "example" for troubled teens today, it might be the adults who go into a business office, a post office or a stock-trading firm and shoot everybody in sight. The school killing sprees match those scenarios far more closely than they resemble the bizarre stories in most video or computer games.

Most Shooters Had Been Bullied

There is one factor that does track reliably through the school shootings in the past few years. In virtually every instance, the teen who did the shooting had been picked on, bullied, ostracized, made the butt of jokes and otherwise given the clear message that he was dirt.

---

1. On March 5, 2001, sixteen-year-old Andy Williams opened fire at Santana High School in San Diego County, killing two people and injuring thirteen.

What's worse, in most cases it wasn't just a handful of brutal hoodlums doing the damage; schoolmates questioned later invariably say that "everybody" thought he was a geek or a weirdo, and had no compunction about letting him know it day after day.

Preventing Bullying

It is important to have [school] policies that clearly address the issue of bullying in all of its forms and that make clear the consequences and procedures that students and adults should follow when there's been a bullying incident.

One of the most successful approaches to dealing with bullying is referred to as "bully-proofing your school." This is a comprehensive approach that involves students, teachers, administrators and parents.

Bully-proofing your school is about changing the very social fabric and climate of the school. It deals with supporting the victims, helping the bullies to change, and changing the silent majority of children who are the bystanders into a caring majority. It involves rewarding positive behaviors, kindness, inclusion.

In schools where it has been implemented, rates of bullying incidences have dropped dramatically.

Adults are the key to dealing with bullying in schools. Students understand clearly what's going on: who the bullies are, who the victims are, [and] how the adults respond to bullying incidences.

Students will take their cues from the adults and will respond accordingly. If we as adults take the time to listen to the students and really find out what is going on and work with the students in bully-proofing a school, we'll find the students cooperating and even helping to lead the program.

"How to Battle the School Bully," November 29, 2001. www.abcnews.com.

Yes, there have always been bullies—but at one time they were themselves objects of disapproval.

The Devastating Impact of Bullying

The majority of kids may not have gone out of their way to be nice to the nerds, but at least they didn't join in the cruelty. It was still, at one time, possible for the victim to think the bullies might have been wrong; today the stigmatization seems to come from everywhere, and he has little hope for escape.

Some people minimize the impact of this, pointing out quite correctly that not all kids who get picked on go to school and kill somebody. So what? Are we saying that as long as there's no homicide involved, bullying is harmless?

What about kids whose confidence is demolished by constant ridicule and abuse, who become completely desocialized, who never develop the ability to form close and lasting relationships? Are we saying we don't care about them as long as they don't shoot anybody?

Teaching Kids to Respect Each Other

There's no "cure" for bullying. But that doesn't mean there's nothing that could be done about it—at least, perhaps, an effort to discourage the more decent majority not to play along.

Based on how little academic learning goes on these days, our schools apparently spend most of their time on programs to boost the self-esteem of their precious little charges, urging them to respect themselves (no matter whether they ever accomplish anything that merits respect). If they've got time for that, why couldn't they make time for programs to teach kids to respect each other?

You won't reach the real bullies, but if you reach the majority who aren't inherently mean, you may leave a window of hope open for the next nerdy kid, who would otherwise think there's nothing left for him but revenge.

> *"The answer to school shootings . . . is to bring good old-fashioned ethics and discipline back to the classroom and the schoolyard."*

School Violence Is the Result of a Lack of Ethics and Discipline in Schools

Daniel G. Jennings

Bullies do not cause school violence, argues Daniel G. Jennings in the following viewpoint. Rather, schools that fail to discipline bullies and instill ethical behavior in students are to blame. Jennings believes that children need to learn to treat fellow students with respect, and should receive meaningful punishments for misbehaving. In addition, he argues, teachers need to stand up to parents who complain about their kids being disciplined. Jennings is a freelance writer and journalist who lives and works in Denver, Colorado. He has worked as a reporter and editor for daily and weekly newspapers in five states.

As you read, consider the following questions:

1. According to Jennings, even though he was bullied as a child, why did he never attack or shoot his fellow students?
2. What types of punishments does the author propose for bad kids in schools?
3. Why do special discipline classes no longer exist in schools, according to Jennings?

In the past few years [since 1999], Americans have been expending a lot of hot air in efforts to determine the cause of school shootings, those terrible incidents where a child—usually a boy—takes a gun to school and guns down his classmates and teachers. The official party line among the nation's media elite is that the cause of these incidents is bullying, that is the teasing and pestering that's a normal part of adolescent life. I, for one, don't buy these claims. The real cause of school shootings is a lack of ethics and discipline in our schools.

Bullying Is Not the Real Cause

I say this because I've had some experience in these matters. I was one of those different kids who had been picked on terribly when I was in school, especially junior high school. I was called names, hit, had garbage thrown at me in class and faced indifference from teachers who didn't care what kids did to each other as long as they didn't disrupt class and school administrators who were as quick to blame the victim as the victimizer. And not once did I consider picking up a gun and shooting my fellow students or attacking them. Even though the teasing once got so bad that I actually ran away from school.

The reason I didn't attack or shoot my fellow students was a simple one. I knew it was wrong to kill and wrong to hit another student simply for calling me a name. My parents raised me right and gave me strong ethical values; those values enabled me to survive the teasing and bullying without picking up a pistol and blowing my classmates away. I hated what the kids were doing to me but even when I was twelve and thirteen, I knew that violence was wrong and refused to engage in it except in self-defense. If another kid took a swing at me or hit me, I hit right back but I didn't beat up every little jerk who called me a name because I knew it was wrong. I knew that what I saw about violence solving problems on TV and at the movies and in comic books was nothing but fantasy.

Teach Kids Ethics and Discipline

So the first thing we must do to prevent school shootings is to teach kids ethics on two levels. First: Teach them that teasing is wrong and that they should have respect for others. In other words teach them the Golden Rule. Do Unto Others as You Would Have Them Do Unto You. Then, teach them that violence is wrong and that violence is not a solution for problems.

Preventing Violence Before It Becomes Serious

While some incidents of serious violence seem to "come out of nowhere," most incidents of school violence or serious disruption start as less serious behavior that accelerate to the point of requiring attention. Many aggressive or disruptive behaviors spiraling out of control might have been defused by early and appropriate responses at the classroom level.

"Preventing School Violence: A Practical Guide to Comprehensive Planning," Indiana Education Policy Center, 2000.

The second thing needed to make our schools safe is discipline. When I was in school, one of the things I wanted most was for the school authorities—the principal or vice principal—to actually discipline the bad kids. To crack down on the bullies, to tell them what they were doing was wrong and make them pay for it. Yet, that rarely happened. Usually what happened was that the principal or guidance counselor would talk to us kids and often blame me as much as the snots who were behaving like little animals. The bad kids rarely got punished. One of the main reasons why bullied kids rarely come forward and report their mistreatment to the principal is that they're just as likely to get a lecture about how they were provoking the bully as to see the bully punished. The bully of course knows this and goes right on bullying.

Bring Back Real Punishments

It's time to bring discipline back to our schools. No, this doesn't mean we bring back the paddle, or expel bad kids when it's time to discipline. Why can't the bad kids be made to clean the bathrooms, mop the halls, pick up trash in the school yard, or wash dishes in the cafeteria. Make the school-yard bully clean the toilets in the boys bathroom, or just write their name on the blackboard a few thousand times? If the jocks are giving the nerds a hard time, why not make the jocks do an extra hundred pushups every day? Such measures wouldn't hurt the bullies but they would quickly teach the bullies to treat their fellow students with respect.

Why not set up special discipline classes or special discipline schools for problem students that are places where those kids can get the extra discipline they need. We used to have such things but we don't anymore because self-proclaimed civil rights activists sued school districts and got moronic judges to rule such things were discriminatory. Naturally, the civil rights attorneys and judges behind these rulings send their kids to private schools where strict old-fashioned discipline is still practiced. (When was the last time you heard of a kid with a gun shooting up a prep school, a parochial school or a Baptist Bible Academy?)

Teachers with Guts

Also, it's time to get a generation of school administrators and school boards with the guts to stand up to parents who complain whenever their kids are disciplined. We also need a generation of parents who are willing to hold school boards, teachers and school administrators accountable for their actions. When was the last time you heard that a principal at a school with a bullying problem getting fired and replaced with a strict disciplinarian who made it clear to the students that teasing would not be tolerated and that those students who tease will be punished?

The answer to school shootings and the discipline problems isn't counseling or sensitivity on the part of teachers and students. The answer is to bring good old-fashioned ethics and discipline back to the classroom and the schoolyard.

"*There is no profile [of a typical school shooter]. Some lived with both parents in 'an ideal, All-American family.' . . . Most had close friends.*"

It Is Impossible to Predict What Will Cause a Child to Commit School Violence

Bill Dedman

In the following viewpoint Bill Dedman presents the findings of Secret Service researchers who have studied the causes of school violence. According to Dedman, there is no common profile of a school shooter; instead, shooters came from both "all-American" families and from broken homes; some were popular and some were loners. Although there is no common profile of school shooters, says Dedman, these youth systematically plan their attacks over many months; thus, observant adults may be able to read the warning signs and intervene. Dedman is a staff reporter for the *Chicago Sun-Times*, one of the ten largest newspapers in the United States.

As you read, consider the following questions:
1. According to Dedman, how did Barry Loukaitis reveal his plans to commit a school shooting?
2. What did the Secret Service learn after studying eighty-three assassins, as explained by the author?
3. What one characteristic do the school shooters share, according to Dedman?

W hat type of kids kill at school?
That's the wrong question, say researchers from the Secret Service.

The people who protect the president have spent the last year [1999] studying the rare but frightening events known as school shootings. The Secret Service studied the cases of 41 children involved in 37 shootings at their current or former school, from 1974 to 2000. It shared its findings with the *Chicago Sun-Times* and plans to publish a guide of advice for schools.

The Secret Service researchers read shooters' journals, letters and poetry. They traveled to prisons to interview 10 of the shooters, who sat for the video camera in orange prison jump suits, all acne and handcuffs, more sad than evil.

"It's real hard to live with the things I've done," said Luke Woodham, now 19, who killed two students in Pearl, Miss., in 1997.

The researchers found that killers do not "snap." They plan. They acquire weapons. They tell others what they are planning. These children take a long, planned, public path toward violence.

No Profile

And there is no profile.

Some lived with both parents in "an ideal, All-American family." Some were children of divorce, or lived in foster homes. A few were loners, but most had close friends.

Few had disciplinary records. Some had honor roll grades and were in Advanced Placement courses; some were failing. Few showed a change in friendships or interest in school.

"What caused these shootings, I don't pretend to know, and I don't know if it's knowable," said Robert A. Fein, a forensic psychologist with the Secret Service. "We're looking for different pieces of the puzzle, not for whether kids wore black clothes."

Looking for a type of child—a profile or checklist of warning signs—doesn't help a principal or teacher or parent who has vague information that raises a concern. Having some of the same traits as school shooters doesn't raise the risk, there being so few cases for comparison.

"Moreover, the use of profiles carries a risk of over-identification," the Secret Service says in its report. "The great majority of students who fit any given profile will not actually pose a risk of targeted violence."

Instead of looking for traits, the Secret Service urges adults to ask more questions, and quickly, about behavior and communication: What has this child said? Does he have grievances? What do his friends know? Does he have access to weapons? Is he depressed or despondent?

These questions are not posed from the traditional law enforcement perspective—has the student broken a rule or law?—or even from a mental health perspective—what is the diagnosis?

Barry Loukaitis

The uselessness of a profile is made clear by Barry Loukaitis, 14, who walked to junior high school on the coldest day of 1996 in Moses Lake, Wash. He wore a black cowboy hat, black clothes, black boots and a black trench coat hiding a .30/.30 rifle underneath. He killed two students and a teacher.

"His behavior did not appear obviously different from that of other early adolescents," wrote a psychiatrist who examined Loukaitis, "until he walked into his junior high school classroom and shot four people, killing three people."

But Loukaitis' behavior was different. He had spoken often, to at least eight friends, for as much as a year, of his desire to kill people.

He had asked his friends how to get ammunition. He had shopped for a long coat to hide the gun; unknowing, his mother took him to seven stores to shop for the right one. He had complained of teasing, but no teacher intervened. His poems were filled with death.

Many teenagers write frightening poetry. Loukaitis also told his friends just what he planned.

"He said that it'd be cool to kill people," one said. "He said he could probably get away with it."

Q. *How long ago was this?*

A. For the last year, probably. I didn't think anything of it.

Q. *And when he showed you the sawed-off shotgun?*

A. I kind of blew that off, too.

The teacher Loukaitis killed, Leona Caires, 49, had written on the report card of the A student: "pleasure to have in class."

The Uselessness of Profiles

Why is the Secret Service studying school shootings?

The Service once believed in profiles. Assassins were presumed to be male, loners, insane. That profile was changed by Squeaky Fromme and Sara Jane Moore, who each tried to kill President Gerald R. Ford in San Francisco in 1975. The night before Moore's attack, the Secret Service had taken away her gun, but she bought another gun and was allowed to approach Ford outside the St. Francis Hotel. She didn't know that her new gun fired high and to the right.

Minds Do Not Just Snap

When someone behaves in a way that violates our expectations, our thinking goes dichotic. Yesterday she was okay; today she's not—normal people and abnormal people, sick folks and well folks. But the human psyche is not like that. Minds don't snap, and nerves don't break down all of a sudden. Figures of speech, often invoked when the behavior of an individual appears to be "out of character," do not explain anything.

When tragic, unbelievable behavior seems to emerge from nowhere, it is inevitably preceded by a process underway for years. In behavioral catastrophes, we tend to medicalize—i.e., to look for an organic origin rather than causes based in experience. We also tend to presume, erroneously, that human behavior is essentially unpredictable.

Lewis P. Lipsitt, *Brown University Child and Adolescent Behavior Letter*, May 2002.

In that same hotel last year [1999], Secret Service agents were briefed on the results of a study by the Service's Protective Intelligence Division. The Service studied all 83 people who tried to kill a public official or celebrity in the United States in the last 50 years.

Assassins, the team found, fit no profile. They rarely threaten. They often change targets. Even if mentally ill, they plan rationally. But because they follow a path toward violence—stalking, acquiring weapons, communicating, acting in ways that concern those around them—it may be possible to intervene.

A National Concern

As the team presented its findings around the country, its audience often made connections to other kinds of targeted violence: workplace attacks, stalking and school shootings.

School violence decreased in the 1990s, but the rare school shootings increased in the 1990s. And then came Columbine High School, where 15 died.[1]

The Service established the National Threat Assessment Center, a sliver of the Secret Service headquarters, just around the corner from Ford's Theater in Washington.

"My hope," said the director of the Secret Service, Brian L. Stafford, "is that the knowledge and expertise utilized by the Secret Service to protect the president may aid our nation's schools and law enforcement communities to safeguard our nation's children."

Putting the Burden on Adults

Kids are kids, of course, not presidential assassins. Fewer of the school shooters show signs of mental illness, which often starts in late adolescence or beyond. The children talk more with peers perhaps testing and probing for the reaction their action will bring.

After seeing that the young shooters didn't just snap, the researchers believe that more responsibility for the shootings rests with adults.

"If kids snap, it lets us off the hook," said Bryan Vossekuil, a former agent on [former] President [Ronald] Reagan's protective detail and executive director of the Service's threat assessment center.

"If you view these shooters as on a path toward violence, it puts the burden on adults. Believing that kids snap is comforting."

Although there is no profile, the shooters do share one characteristic.

1. In April 1999 two students went on a shooting spree at this Littleton, Colorado, high school.

"I believe they're all boys because the way we bring up boys in America predisposes them to a sense of loneliness and disconnection and sadness," said William S. Pollack, a psychologist and consultant to the Secret Service.

"When they have additional pain, additional grievances, they are less likely to reach out and talk to someone, less likely to be listened to. Violence is the only way they start to feel they can get a result."

Periodical Bibliography

The following articles have been selected to supplement the diverse views presented in this chapter.

Jeffrey Fagan
"Policing Guns and Youth Violence," *Future of Children*, Summer/Fall 2002.

Aimee Howd
"How to Stop Kids from Killing Kids," *Insight on the News*, April 24, 2000.

Issues and Controversies on File
"Video Games and Violence," February 13, 2004.

Richard Jerome
"Disarming the Rage: Across the Country, Thousands of Students Stay Home from School Each Day, Terrified of Humiliation or Worse at the Hands of Bullies," *People Weekly*, June 4, 2001.

Joy Bennett Kinnon
"Why Children Are Killing Children—African American Juvenile Crime," *Ebony*, January 1, 1999.

Carolyn Kleiner
"Breaking the Cycle," *U.S. News & World Report*, April 29, 2002.

Legal Affairs
"Root Causes," September 2003.

Lewis Lipsitt
"Behavior Develops, Minds Don't Snap," *Brown University Child and Adolescent Behavior Letter*, May 2002.

Ian Murray
"Juvenile Murders: Guns the Least of It," *Christian Science Monitor*," March 27, 2000.

Mark O'Keefe
"Lessons of Columbine," *San Diego Union-Tribune*, April 16, 2000.

Ann Patchett
"The Age of Innocence," *New York Times Magazine*, September 29, 2002.

Mark Peplow
"Full of Goodness," *New Scientist*, November 16, 2002.

Carla Rivera
"Report Links Crime to Bad Child Care," *Los Angeles Times*, March 15, 2001.

Bruce Shapiro
"The Guns of Littleton," *Nation*, May 17, 1999.

Ray Wisher
"Joined at the Hip—Drugs and Crime," *American Enterprise*, June 1, 2001.

CHAPTER 2

How Should the Criminal Justice System Treat Juvenile Offenders?

Chapter Preface

In the March 2000 election, California voters passed Proposition 21, a measure that allows the criminal justice system in that state to impose stricter penalties on juvenile criminals. Under Proposition 21 juveniles are subject to increased punishment for many offenses, including gang-related crimes, robbery, carjacking, and drive-by shootings. The measure also requires adult trials for juveniles fourteen or older charged with murder or specified sex offenses, and it eliminates informal probation for juveniles who commit felonies.

Proponents of the proposition argue that juvenile crime has become increasingly prevalent and violent, and that harsher punishments are needed to protect society and deter youth from committing crimes. According to district attorney Michael D. Bradbury, "Times have changed. Juvenile truancy has been replaced with violent rape and murder. We need to adapt the law so that youths who commit adult crime do adult time." In Bradbury's opinion, Proposition 21 deters juvenile crime by sending a "clear message to kids" that if they commit a crime, they will be severely punished. Advocates Maggie Elvey, Grover Trask, and Richard Tefank echo Bradbury's claim that the most effective deterrent to youth crime is the threat of harsh punishment. They state:

> Ask yourself if a violent gang member believes the worst punishment he might receive for a gang-ordered murder is incarceration at the California Youth Authority [youth correction facility] until age 25, will that stop him from taking a life? Of course not. . . . Proposition 21 ends the "slap on the wrist" of current law by imposing real consequences for GANG MEMBERS, RAPISTS AND MURDERERS who cannot be reached through prevention or education.

However, there are many analysts who believe that the harsher punishments mandated by Proposition 21 are not a good solution to juvenile crime, and may even make it worse. "Children have a bigger capacity to change than adults," maintains journalist Terrie Albano, "and therefore the justice system, especially for juveniles, should have the goal of help and rehabilitation." Activists Lavonne McBroom, Gail Dryden, and Raymond Wingerd point out that harsh treatment of young criminals is likely only to increase their criminal activity. They state: "In prison, without the treatment and education available in the juvenile system, [juveniles] will be confined in institutions housing adult criminals. What will these young people learn in state prison—how to be better criminals?"

California is not the only state that has begun to impose harsher penalties on young criminals. Various measures across the nation have been proposed to help states "get tough" on these youth. Like Proposition 21, these measures have all provoked heated argument. The authors in the following chapter explore some of the controversial issues that surround the trying and sentencing of juvenile criminals.

> "When young criminals kill and rape, they
> should be treated like adults, even
> executing them!"

Juvenile Offenders Should Be Eligible for the Death Penalty

Don Boys

In the following viewpoint Don Boys argues that the juvenile criminal justice system is too lenient. Youth violence is not the result of bad parents or societal pressures, maintains Boys; children choose to commit crimes. He believes that violent youth should be held accountable for their actions and advocates harsh punishments for juvenile criminals, including the death penalty for serious crimes. Boys is a former member of the Indiana House of Representatives and author of thirteen books. He also wrote columns for *USA Today* for eight years.

As you read, consider the following questions:

1. How many cases of juvenile crime do the courts handle every year, according to Boys?
2. What does the "fallen nature" of youth mean, in the author's opinion?
3. How does Boys respond to the argument that poverty causes juvenile crime?

O ur city streets are dark, dirty, dangerous and are often dominated by raping, robbing and rampaging children. Each year juvenile courts handle thousands of criminal homicides and over a million cases of lesser crimes. We are seeing more and more very young people commit serious, sordid and sadistic crimes—some kids as young as six! As families, homes and churches implode, a subculture of juvenile criminals has developed.

A Serious Problem

Juveniles used to be considered young, athletic, students with ruddy complexions, squeaky voices and acne, but now they are often vindictive, vicious and violent criminals.

We have been assured that "there is no such thing as a bad boy" (or girl); however, the fact is, there is no such thing as a good boy (or girl). No kid has to be taught to lie, steal, talk back, rebel, etc. It is human nature. Theologians call it the "fallen nature," as a result of original sin. But since that is not politically correct, men have been conned into believing all people are basically good—then we try to justify and explain why "good" people commit outrageously brutal crimes.

Part of the problem of juvenile crime is the criminal justice system itself. While ours may be the "best in the world" (what does that say about the rest of the world?) it is long overdue for a major overhaul. . . .

No More Free Rides

Kids must no longer have a free ride until age 18. They must get the message that they will be held accountable for their actions with their names and photos published in the media, and their record following them if they continue into adult crime. Studies show that a juvenile's crime record is one of the most valid predictors of repeat adult crime.

Young criminals should not be in school, and while the bleeding hearts whine about those kids, I prefer to show my concern for the large group who wants to learn. Put the violent kids in a boot camp where they can be made into "young marines" under the tutelage of a traditional leatherneck trained at Parris Island [military installation near Beaufort, South Carolina].

Get them up at 5:00 A.M., feed them a big breakfast and work them until they drop. Absolutely no back talk and only magic words such as "yes sir," "no sir," "please," and "thank you, sir" would be permitted. And no psychologist, psychiatrist, social worker or lawyer within 100 miles!

Minimum Age for Death Penalty Eligibility

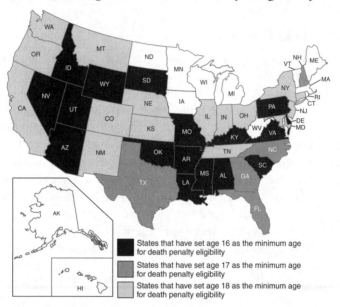

States that have set age 16 as the minimum age for death penalty eligibility

States that have set age 17 as the minimum age for death penalty eligibility

States that have set age 18 as the minimum age for death penalty eligibility

In *Thompson. v. Oklahoma* (1988), the Supreme Court ruled that it is unconstitutional to execute offenders who were age 15 or under when they committed their crimes. Of the 38 states that allow the death penalty for certain forms of murder, 17 have set a minimum age of 16. Sixteen states and the federal government require offenders to be at least 18 years old at the time of their crime to be eligible for the death penalty. While some critics contend that the execution of juvenile offenders constitutes cruel and unusual punishment, others have argued that the minimum age should be lowered to 15.

Office of Juvenile Justice and Deliquency Prevention, 2002.

Those kids who are involved in nonviolent crime would be treated less severely. They would be forced to make restitution to their victims, clean up any mess they made and spend time in structured community service.

Kids must learn that justice will be swift, sure and severe in the courts if not at home and school. Personal accountability will be the reality from now on. That will appall many social scientists and psychologists who tell us that a person is not responsible for personal actions. It all goes back, we are told, to poor potty training, low self-esteem, poor living conditions, etc., so a young person should not be held to an accounting for his crimes. My intellectual reply is poppycock, balderdash and a generous portion of hogwash.

We are told that kids murder, mug and maim because they grew up in poverty; however, poverty doesn't cause crime; crime causes poverty. Juveniles, like adults, commit crimes because they choose to do so. And they must be held accountable.

Serious Punishments Are Necessary

When young criminals kill and rape, they should be treated like adults, even executing them! Most of us are horrified at that thought but if capital punishment can be defended (and it can be) then who is to say one must be 21? If a 16-year-old commits a vicious murder, who says he should not pay with his life? Of course, there must be an age below which a child would not be executed, but that is a political decision made in each state.

So the message to kids should be clear, concise and conclusive. No free ride until 18. No anonymity. No blaming poverty, parents or potty training for criminality. No more community service for rape and murder. Even the most dull teen will understand that society considers leniency lunacy and a thing of the past.

Kids think they can get away with murder and they will continue to believe that until citizens force the criminal justice system to get its act together. When a few teens "walk the last mile" other teens will get the message that sane, sensible and scared people are taking over from the bleeding hearts.

The radical leftist, upon reading this, will stand up and on cue, bleed all over himself; however, my heart bleeds for the innocent victims not for criminals, young or old.

"When we execute juvenile offenders, we ignore what we know . . . about the many ways in which children and adolescents are different from adults."

Juvenile Offenders Should Not Be Eligible for the Death Penalty

Steven A. Drizin and Stephen K. Harper

In the following viewpoint Steven A. Drizin and Stephen K. Harper argue that because juvenile criminals' ethical development is incomplete, they do not deserve the same criminal punishments as adults, and should not be eligible for the death penalty. Rehabilitation is more effective for young offenders than for adults, maintain Drizin and Harper, and should be the preferred method of dealing with young criminals. According to the authors, the United States needs to join the majority of nations around the world that have banned the harmful practice of executing youth. Drizin is the supervising attorney of the Children and Family Justice Center at Northwestern University's School of Law in Illinois. Harper is an attorney and adjunct professor at the University of Miami School of Law in Florida.

As you read, consider the following questions:
1. What is a "superpredator," as defined by Drizin and Harper?
2. What international agreements forbid the death penalty for youth, according to the authors?

On February 1 [2000], Rome was treated to a brilliant spectacle when the Colosseum—a place where ancient Romans came to watch condemned men fight to the death—was bathed in golden light. The United Nations, the city of Rome and the Vatican have converted the Colosseum into a symbol for a worldwide campaign to abolish the death penalty. Now it is illuminated for 48 hours whenever someone—anywhere in the world—is spared from execution. On this occasion, the Colosseum was lit to celebrate Illinois Gov. George Ryan's moratorium on the death penalty.[1]

While the Illinois moratorium is indeed a bright spot in the recent U.S. history with the death penalty, the Colosseum lights were extinguished throughout most of January [2000], as 12 executions were carried out in the United States. The darkest hours of all occurred during the executions of three young men who committed their crimes when they were younger than 18.

America's continued practice of executing juvenile offenders has alarming implications for our society's visions of morality, crime and punishment, conformance to international law and indeed childhood itself. When we execute juvenile offenders, we ignore what we know—and what science continues to teach us—about the many ways in which children and adolescents are different from adults. We ignore long-established principles of law holding that punishment should be commensurate not simply with the criminal act, but with the intent, culpability and mitigating factors pertaining to the individual offender. We ignore what the American Society for Adolescent Psychiatry tells us: Adolescents who "commit capital crimes very often suffer from serious psychological and family disturbances which exacerbate their already existing vulnerabilities."

Moreover, executing juvenile offenders is a barbaric and atavistic practice that makes the United States—long a champion of human rights—a pariah nation in the eyes of the world. It exposes us as hypocrites with respect to both our foreign and domestic policy. How, for example, can we impose economic sanctions against human rights violators abroad when we are

---

1. In 2000 Ryan stopped all executions in Illinois.

violating international law and the human rights of children at home? How can we hold troubled adolescents fully accountable for their crimes while legally preventing them—because of their immaturity—from entering contracts, making medical decisions, joining the military, voting, smoking, drinking alcohol or even gaining admission to an "R" rated movie?

Juvenile Offenders on Death Row

The Commonwealth of Virginia rang in the new millennium by executing Douglas Christopher Thomas on January 10 [2000] and Steven Roach just three days later. Texas, which has executed eight juvenile offenders since 1973 and currently [in 2000] has 28 youthful offenders on death row, executed Glenn McGinnis on January 25. These executions were carried out notwithstanding appeals from numerous organizations, including the European Union and the American Bar Association. Even Pope John Paul II sent a plea to [former] Gov. George W. Bush asking that he commute McGinnis' sentence to life in prison.

About 73 other juvenile offenders are awaiting execution on death rows throughout the United States. More than two-thirds of them are minorities. Fifty-one percent are black, 18 percent are Latino and 31 percent are white. All are male.

Other juveniles will continue to take up temporary residence on death rows. Out of the 38 death penalty states, 19 execute 16- and 17-year-olds and four execute those 17 and older. In 1988, the U.S. Supreme Court held that executing children under the age of 16 violated the Eighth Amendment's ban against "cruel and unusual punishment" because it is contrary to "evolving standards of decency that mark the progress of a maturing society."

If not for this decision, some states would be executing even younger offenders. Former Gov. Pete Wilson, the architect of California's recently passed Proposition 21,[2] has floated the idea that the age for the death penalty should be lowered to 14. In the wake of the Jonesboro, Ark., school shooting two years ago,[3] Texas legislator Jim Pitts proposed lowering the age to 11.

2. Proposition 21, passed in 2000, creates tougher penalties for juvenile offenders.
3. In 1998 four students and one teacher were killed, and ten students wounded in this Arkansas shooting.

America's unforgiving attitude toward youth in the justice system is a stunning indication of just how far our country has tumbled from its leadership role in treating troubled children. More than a century ago, America led the world in its thinking about how to treat young people in trouble with the law by creating the world's first juvenile court.

Outraged by the treatment of children in adult prisons and jails and following the lessons of the nascent human sciences, reformers created a system and laws that recognized that children and adolescents were different than adults. Policymakers recognized that childhood, especially adolescence, was a transitional period of life where cognitive abilities, judgment, impulse control, identity and emotions are still being developed. They recognized that the malleability of youth makes juvenile offenders inherently capable of rehabilitation.

A Cruel System

Glen McGinnis was nine years old the first time he was raped by his stepfather. His mother, a crack addict and a prostitute, offered little in the way of parenting. He was beaten with an electrical cord and a baseball bat, and burned with hot grease. When Glen was 17, he shot and killed a laundry attendant and was subsequently executed by the state of Texas.

His case is symptomatic of the cruel and unjustified manner by which the system of capital punishment in the United States fails to distinguish between children and adults.

Sue Gunawardena-Vaughn, *People's Weekly World*, November 16, 2002.

In creating juvenile courts, Americans also understood the basic truth that adolescents are simply less culpable than adults for their misdeeds. Adults are presumed to be fully formed moral actors capable of understanding right from wrong, of choosing between the two and conforming their actions to the requirements of the law. However, because children and adolescents are still maturing and do not possess the same capacities, judgment and controls, and because they are often traumatized and abused, we have not generally punished them as fully as we do an adult who has committed the same act.

The last two decades, however, have witnessed enormous changes in the way our justice system treats offenders, first in the adult system and more recently, in the juvenile justice system. As a result of punitive measures such as "three strikes" laws, "sexual predator" laws,[4] the abolishment of parole and mandatory prison sentences, currently more than 2 million Americans are behind bars. The adult system is now focused on punishing and incapacitating offenders and has all but given up on trying to rehabilitate them.

In the last decade, these "get tough" measures have also come to drive juvenile justice policy, destroying much of the historical differences between the two systems and placing the juvenile court's rehabilitative ethos in jeopardy. Between 1992 and 1997, 47 states passed laws making it easier to try children as adults.

Superpredator Myth

What spurred these changes? The late 1980s and early 1990s did see an alarming increase in the number of juveniles charged with murder. As crack cocaine hit the streets in America's urban areas, adult gang leaders and drug dealers recruited and armed youngsters in their battle to control the lucrative drug trade. This spike in homicide arrests was almost exclusively confined to the inner cities and virtually all of the increase was gun-related.

This increased violence among urban teens was cause for concern but did not justify the wholesale demonization of America's youth that soon followed. Beginning in late 1995, Princeton professor John DiIulio coined the word "superpredator" to describe a new breed of "remorseless and morally impoverished" juveniles who would soon flood America's streets as projected increases in the youth population came to pass. Politicians seized on this rhetoric, inflamed the public's fear and exploited the gap between public perception and the reality of juvenile crime. Increased press coverage of juvenile violence, making it seem like the norm rather than an aberration, also fanned public hysteria.

The truth is that less than one-half of 1 percent of America's kids were arrested for a violent crime last year [1999]. And

4. "Three strikes" laws mandate long periods of punishment for persons convicted of a felony on three or more separate occasions. "Sexual predator" laws mandate long periods of punishment for habitual sexual offenders.

even though we've had seven straight years of declining juvenile crime during a time when the overall population of youth has grown—trends that completely discredit the superpredator myth—juvenile crime remains a hot-button political issue today. California's Proposition 21 is the most recent example of this trend and signals that there may be no end in sight.

The effect of these changes has altered the landscape of juvenile justice. Twenty-three states now have no bottom age limit for kids to be tried as adults. Last year, Nathaniel Abraham, a Michigan boy who was only 11 at the time he was charged with murder, became the youngest boy in modern American history to be prosecuted as an adult. According to Amnesty International, Nathaniel was just one of more than 200,000 youngsters under the age of 18 who were prosecuted in our adult courts last year.

Perhaps the most disturbing result of these changes, however, is the increase in the number of children housed in adult prisons. Just this month [April 2000], the Bureau of Justice Statistics reported that the number of youths under the age of 17 who were committed to adult prisons has more than doubled, rising from 3,400 in 1985 to 7,400 in 1997. More than a quarter of these youths in adult prisons are between the ages of 13 and 16.

The dismantling of the juvenile justice system demonstrates that attention and focus have shifted away from the individual child's needs, problems, strengths, developmental stage, potential and culpability. Now the focus simply is on the seriousness of the crime and meting out punishment. We no longer care who or how old the offender is, what his intent was, why he is in trouble, who he may yet become, or what extenuating factors may have contributed to the act.

This singular obsession for retribution is also what drives the decision to execute juvenile offenders. Thus, notwithstanding the fact that Chris Thomas was an extremely troubled adolescent who suffered from depression and abused substances, Virginia Gov. Jim Gilmore focused only on the need to "demand complete accountability" when denying Thomas' final plea for clemency. Similarly, the fact that Glenn McGinnis had been raped by his stepfather when he was 9 and was later beaten with a baseball bat and burned with hot grease by his mother and stepfather fell on Gov. Bush's deaf ears. Rather, Bush insisted on sending "a strong message that the consequences of violent criminal behavior will be swift and sure. . . ." The fact that Thomas and McGinnis were only 17 at the time of their crimes has become irrelevant.

The United States Shuns International Standards

America's changing visions of punishment and childhood—most dramatically illustrated by this practice of executing juvenile offenders—are increasingly out of step with international standards of decency and established international law. All but the United States and the collapsed state of Somalia have ratified the 10-year-old U.N. Convention on the Rights of the Child, which forbids the death penalty against youths under 18. Similarly, the International Covenant on Civil and Political Rights, which has more than 144 signatory countries, also bans the execution of those who commit crimes under the age of 18. Deferring to the rights of its individual states, the United States specifically reserved its right to ignore the covenant's ban on executing juveniles.

Over the last decade, only six other countries are known to have executed juvenile offenders—Yemen, China, Iran, Nigeria, Pakistan and Saudi Arabia. China and Yemen have recently outlawed the practice. In the 1990s, Amnesty International documented 19 cases of child offenders who were executed. Ten were executed in the United States alone—more than all the remaining countries combined. In this fundamental area of human rights, the United States has gone from a leader to an outlaw. . . .

The great Russian novelist and philosopher, Fyodor Dostoevsky, once wrote that a society should be "judged not by how it treats its outstanding citizens but by how it treats its criminals." We believe that an even better barometer of a nation's soul is how it treats its most troubled children. In executing juvenile offenders, America has fallen from grace.

By stopping this shameful practice, America can take a significant stride toward once again establishing itself as a beacon for the world in the area of children's and human rights. Until that happens, we'll have to look to the Colosseum for our hope and inspiration.

| "*Adult detention facilities are probably better equipped to deal with the type of dangerous and violent juvenile offenders we are seeing today.*"

Adult Prisons Are Sometimes Appropriate for Juveniles

James C. Backstrom

With the number of juvenile crimes at historic highs, it makes sense to house some juvenile criminals in adult detention facilities, which are more numerous than juvenile detention centers, argues James C. Backstrom in the following viewpoint. In Backstrom's opinion, housing juveniles with adults would not be harmful. In fact, he maintains, serious and violent juvenile criminals might be more effectively punished in the adult justice system than the juvenile one. Backstrom is a Dakota County, Minnesota, attorney. He is responsible for prosecuting all levels of crime committed by juveniles within Dakota County.

As you read, consider the following questions:

1. According to Backstrom, what do census projections show about the juvenile population in the United States?
2. How have juvenile offenders changed over the last twenty to thirty years, in the author's opinion?
3. How have some of the federal regulatory restrictions governing the detention of juvenile offenders been eased, according to Backstrom?

The availability of juvenile detention facilities to deal with youth apprehended for violent crime is a significant problem in most areas of this country. In 1991, there were over 120,000 juveniles arrested in the United States for violent crime. It was estimated that there were just under 48,000 secure beds available to house those offenders. In my home jurisdiction, a county of about 320,000 people in the southeast Twin Cities metro area [Minnesota], we currently [2000] do not have a detention facility. In the last five years we have experienced dramatic increases in the number of juveniles charged with criminal conduct. Without a juvenile detention facility we have had to ship juvenile offenders who have been apprehended for murder, attempted murder and other violent crimes as far away as 250 miles to find available detention space. In some cases, juveniles who should have been detained to protect the public safety have simply been sent home on electronic home monitoring. While this has occurred, we have often had available detention beds in our county jail or at local police lock-ups. However, strict federal and state regulations prohibit the housing of juvenile offenders in adult facilities, even for relatively short periods of time.

The numbers of serious, violent and habitual juvenile offenders in need of detention space have risen dramatically over the last 5 years in America. Census projections also reflect a growth in juvenile population of close to 20% in the United States between 1990 and 2010. In my jurisdiction, we project an increase of over 60% in the number of youth between 14–17 over the next 15 years. Even if juvenile arrest rates do not continue to grow as they have for most of the last decade, the overall number of juvenile crimes committed will likely be dramatically higher in the next 20 years given these population trends. An ominous forecast indeed.

Common Sense to Use Adult Facilities

Sound public policy dictates that serious, violent and habitual offenders need to be incarcerated to protect the public safety and provide appropriate levels of punishment and accountability. Common sense dictates that using available space in local county jails and state prisons should be an available option, subject to reasonable restrictions. In fact, adult detention facilities are probably better equipped to deal with the type of dangerous and violent juvenile offenders we are seeing today than are most juvenile detention facilities. Why shouldn't we be able to take advantage of existing detention facilities, with staffs trained in managing serious and dangerous offenders, whenever possible?

It needs to be kept in mind that many of the concerns about poor conditions and untrained staff in local jails throughout America that were part of the initial reasons which led to establishing strict regulation of juvenile detention facilities, have long been corrected. We also cannot overlook the fact that the juvenile criminal offender we see throughout America today bears little resemblance to the juvenile offender seen 20–30 years ago. We are in many circumstances dealing with sophisticated, often gang connected, juvenile criminals committing crimes of violence with dangerous weapons. There are certainly fewer reasons today to be overly concerned about segregating these hard core juvenile offenders from adult offenders as there were 25 years ago. I am not suggesting that we lock up every juvenile needing incarceration with hardened adult criminals and gang members. What I am suggesting is that local law enforcement officials be given greater flexibility in making the decision as to when and under what conditions housing serious and violent juvenile offenders in adult lock-ups is appropriate.

Easy to Implement

Most modern adult jails and prisons have segregated units to allow separation of offenders by categories, such as pretrial/post-trial or men/women. These facilities can also easily segregate offenders by age groups. As one of my colleagues recently pointed out to me, juveniles aged 15–17 can be mandated by law to attend the same schools as young adults aged 18–19, but they are absolutely prohibited from being housed in a detention facility with the same young adults if they commit a crime. The fact of the matter is that in many cases the 16 year old offender was a partner with the 18 year old offender in committing the offense that led to his incarceration in the first place.

Many juvenile offenders who have committed serious and

Changing Goals in the Juvenile Justice System

[The] concept of a distinct justice system for juveniles focused upon treatment has come under attack in recent years. Beginning in the late 1980s, communities across the nation began to experience dramatically increased rates of juvenile crime. The arrest rate for violent crimes of both males and females began to increase in 1987 and continued to escalate until the mid-1990s. Although this trend appears to have reversed, rates of serious crimes committed by juveniles remain well above historical levels.

The increasing incidence and severity of crimes committed by juveniles led many to question the efficacy of the juvenile court system and to call for a harsher response to juvenile crime. Juvenile delinquency that results in serious offenses has come to be viewed as more a criminal problem than a behavioral problem, resulting in a shift in public response to the management of juvenile offenders. Researchers have noted this shift in trends toward more arrests, longer periods of incarceration, fewer opportunities for rehabilitation, and, most significantly, increases in the transfer of juveniles to the adult criminal justice system.

Juveniles are increasingly placed in adult correctional facilities. Concerned that the juvenile justice system may be ill equipped to handle youth charged with serious crimes and that the juvenile court may be too lenient in its punishment and control of such youth, many states have begun amending their criminal codes so that youth charged with certain crimes can be tried in adult courts and sentenced as adults.

Bureau of Justice Assistance, "Juveniles in Adult Prisons and Jails: A National Assessment," October 2000.

violent crimes can and should be prosecuted as adults for their offenses, thereby eliminating the current legal restrictions concerning detention of these offenders in adult facilities. However, some of these offenders will not be prosecuted as adults and even those who are ultimately dealt with in adult court must be detained prior to the transfer of their case to the adult system. It certainly seems reasonable to me to allow local corrections officials the discretion to house serious, violent and habitual juvenile offenders in adult lockups if space is available and if it can be managed to insure as much segregation of juvenile and adult populations as possible. Clearly, it seems appropriate in any case to allow juveniles charged or convicted of similar crimes as are young adults between 18–25 to be housed together. Co-located juvenile and adult detention facilities, utilizing shared staff and joint use of recreational/lunch and open areas, are cost effective and should also be permitted.

Some Progress Is Being Made

Some easing of federal regulatory restrictions in this area have already occurred. Last year [1999], regulations enacted by the Office of Juvenile Justice and Delinquency Prevention (OJJDP) did in fact ease some of the restrictions relating to sight and sound separation; co-location of juvenile and adult detention facilities, and immediate detention before and after court appearances. I am pleased with the direction of the leadership now being exhibited in the OJJDP, as they seek to cope with how best to deal with the new breed of juvenile criminal seen today. Clearly, a balanced approach, of appropriately holding serious, violent and habitual juvenile offenders accountable for their crimes and looking for every available means to prevent these crimes from occurring in the first place, is needed. These efforts are not incompatible—in fact they compliment one another—and both protect the public safety. Common sense and sound financial planning also dictate that we further re-examine state and federal legislative restrictions dealing with the joint housing of adult and juvenile criminal offenders. Greater flexibility is needed at the local level to make determinations of when, under what conditions, and how long it is appropriate to house juvenile offenders with adults.

"Incarcerated youths run a great risk of being assaulted by adult inmates and adult prisons become schools of crime for these youngsters."

Juveniles Should Not Be Placed in Adult Prisons

J. Steven Smith

Incarcerating juvenile criminals with adults is both ineffective and harmful, maintains J. Steven Smith in the following viewpoint. According to Smith, youth in adult prisons are likely to be assaulted and are also likely to commit more crimes when released. Further, argues Smith, the desire to incarcerate juveniles with adults is based on the public's fear that juvenile crime is increasing; however, crimes committed by youth are actually decreasing. He advocates treatment rather than incarceration for young criminals. Smith is professor of justice education at Taylor University in Fort Wayne, Indiana.

As you read, consider the following questions:
1. According to Smith, what does the story of the twelve-year-old boy in the maximum-security prison reveal about children who commit criminal acts?
2. What is the likelihood of a juvenile in adult prison being assaulted, according to Ronnie Greene and Geoff Dougherty?
3. What type of juvenile crime is particularly well-suited to the restorative justice model, in Smith's opinion?

J. Steven Smith, "Adult Prisons: No Place for Kids," *USA Today*, vol. 131, July 2002, p. 34. Copyright © 2002 by the Society for the Advancement of Education. Reproduced by permission.

S everal years ago, one of the news feature shows on tele- vision had an interviewer talking with a freckle-faced, redheaded 12-year-old boy. The interview was taking place in a maximum-security prison yard.

When asked what he had done to warrant being in the prison, the youngster related how he had been spotted by lo- cal police as he drove a stolen car. After a high-speed chase, he crashed into an interstate highway roadblock. Several state and local law enforcement agencies and dozens of po- lice cars were involved.

The interviewer asked if the child was sorry for what he had done because it had resulted in a sentence to an adult maximum-security prison. The boy responded that he would do it again because it was the "greatest day" of his life!

"It was just like 'Smokey and the Bandit' [a popular chase film]!" the boy effused. Clearly, he continued after a period of months to be caught up in the childish excitement of his crim- inal act. A mature sorrow for his actions and the resulting pun- ishment were absent. Children are immature by definition.

A Policy That Harms Juveniles

This practice of locking up young people with adult criminals harkens back to the policies of the 1700s, when offenders, re- gardless of age, were thrown together in poorhouses and workhouses. The results were predictable. The young people got worse as a result of exposure to the more-hardened crim- inals. It is hard to believe that, with the amount of scientific evidence we have generated over the last 100 years, political leaders still believe it is a good idea to lock misbehaving chil- dren up with adult criminals.

Today, there are thousands of young people living desper- ate lives locked away in adult prisons. Across the nation, the U.S. Department of Justice estimates there were about 5,500 juveniles being held in adult prisons in the late 1990s. There is little doubt that there are more than that now [in 2002]. Additionally, there are over 9,000 youths being held in the nation's adult jails.

While most of us would expect that youths in adult prisons were the most-violent and dangerous juvenile offenders, the Department of Justice reported that 39% of the juveniles in adult prisons were sentenced for a nonviolent offense. The most-serious charge for almost 40% of these young Americans was most likely a drug or nonviolent property offense. It is reasonable to propose that seriously violent youths should be held in adult facilities only if they are incapable of being effectively managed in a juvenile facility.

In 1980, Congress passed amendments to the Juvenile Justice and Delinquency Prevention Act of 1974. Chief among these amendments was a requirement to separate juveniles from adults in the nation's jails. This required local jails absolutely to prevent juveniles from seeing or hearing adult offenders. This provision was strictly enforced and required the restructuring of supervision for more than 6,000 juveniles in Indiana alone, for instance. This amendment is still on the books in spite of the ever-increasing use of adult prisons and jails for juvenile offenders.

Unfounded Fear of Juveniles

Many juvenile justice experts believe that locking away youngsters in adult prisons is a response formed out of panic and fear. As [professor] William J. Chambliss states in *Power, Politics, and Crime*, "Panic over youth crime is as persistent in western society as is worry about the stock market, but, like so many other alarms, it is based on political and law enforcement propaganda, not facts." In the late 1990s, another spate of law enforcement–driven propaganda about the "time bomb" of juvenile crime blossomed. That campaign was closely linked to the creation of anxiety over the state of the family in the U.S., where children were said to be growing up "fatherless, jobless, and godless," dependent on "welfare moms."

Elected officials realized that the public wanted something done about the "crime epidemic" that people believed was afflicting the nation. Rather than tell the public that there was not a crime wave, politicians responded with a great effort to "punish offenders back to righteousness." Not only has it been proven beyond any doubt that long prison terms do not reduce the crime rate, but elected officials failed to tell the public that they were safer than they had been since the 1960s. Juvenile crime—in fact, all crime—has been in decline over the last several years.

The percentage of crimes attributable to juveniles has remained stable at just under 20% since the 1980s. There is no scientific reason for a special effort directed at juvenile crime, but there certainly are political advantages to building up crime as a major social problem. "Although the number of juveniles arrested remained relatively stable over the 1990s, there has been an unending public diatribe about the increasing danger posed by juvenile crime," according to [writer] Albert J. Mehan in "The Organizational Career of a Statistic: Gang Statistics and the Politics of Policing Gangs," a 1998 report to the Office of Juvenile Justice and Delinquency Prevention.

Adult Prison Is Not an Effective Deterrent

The calls from elected officials and law enforcement agencies have been loud and clear. They argue that there is a "tidal wave of juvenile crime" at the edge of American cities and it is threatening to overwhelm communities unless there are tough new laws and penalties to dissuade juvenile offenders. Thus, they maintain, there is only one thing that officials see as a "real" deterrent to juvenile criminals, and that is the adult prison, which is almost universally viewed to be the most serious response available to legislators who are concerned about punishing crime.

In March, 2001, *The Pittsburgh Post-Gazette* reported on the "new era" that was begun in the mid 1990s. The politicians promised a tough new policy of cracking down on violent juvenile criminals. No more would "brutal teenagers be coddled" by juvenile courts, thereby encouraging additional misbehavior.

This idea is not supported by the literature on juvenile delinquency. A juvenile offender is typically placed under the supervision of the juvenile court until the age of majority (18-21, depending on the state). Adult courts that try juvenile offenders are often less likely to require intensive treatment and will often call for a much shorter period of court supervision. The juvenile offender looks at the shorter "sentence" from the adult court as a "free pass" to commit additional illegal acts.

Legislators even outlawed the traditional fact-finding role of the judge. The Building Blocks for Youth Initiative reports that youths who are tried as adults are not being waived to adult court by the traditional judicial review of the particular facts. Instead, prosecutors or legislators are making 85% of these critical decisions. This practice does not allow a full airing of the facts in a juvenile case and therefore hurts the cause of justice. So, legislators sought not only to treat juveniles more harshly in adult court, but removed the traditional oversight protections of the courtroom judge.

Margulies. © 1996 by *The Record, New Jersey*, JimMarg@aol.com. Reproduced by permission of Jimmy Margulies.

According to the MacArthur Research Network on Adolescent Development and Juvenile Justice, "From a developmental perspective, many youths do not have the cognitive, emotional, and social maturity that they will have when they are adults. Moreover, considerable evidence has indicated higher prevalence of mental disorders among youths who come before the courts than among youths in general, including developmental delays, mental illnesses, and mental retardation."

High Risk of Assault

It is not uncommon to see juveniles "showing tough" when they first arrive at any correctional institution, but when they do that at an adult maximum-security institution, it can have disastrous results. As [journalists] Ronnie Greene and Geoff Dougherty reported in the *Miami Herald* on Sept. 7, 2001, "Florida's youngest prison inmates are also its most likely victims of reported assaults."

They indicated that juveniles locked up in adult male prisons are four times more likely than adults to report being assaulted, and 21 times more likely to be assaulted than teens held in one of Florida's secure juvenile facilities. They also pointed out the likelihood that one-half of these improperly placed juveniles will be assaulted while incarcerated.

[Journalist] Barbara White Stack of the *Pittsburgh Post-Gazette* (March 18, 2001) reported a similar failure of the "get tough on kids" program in Pennsylvania. She noted that these new get-tough laws have been described as being "both unfair and ineffective," increasing the probability a youth would "commit new crimes," and making youths "more likely to commit more serious new offenses."

The children who have been charged with "adult crimes" are among the most vulnerable youngsters in the nation. Of those charged as adults in Pennsylvania, "more than half had suffered abuse or neglect as children, and at least 40% were the children of criminals."

The new get-tough laws aimed at punishing juveniles have been implemented and found wanting on a number of fronts. First, these laws are unnecesary. Juvenile crime is decreasing, and youths continue to represent a small percentage of the crime rate. Almost half of the juveniles who are locked away in dangerous adult prisons committed a nonviolent crime which could be effectively addressed by the juvenile courts. Second, these laws injure young people. Incarcerated youths run a great risk of being assaulted by adult inmates and adult prisons become schools of crime for these youngsters.

Alternatives to Adult Prison

Based on scientific research and common sense, there are many ideas that will address juvenile crime in a cost-effective fashion while maximizing community safety. There are dozens of organizations across the nation capable of assisting elected officials in the development of more-reasonable responses to juvenile misbehavior. Some well-researched ideas that have been proposed by these groups include:

First and foremost, it is critical for society to move away from the current punishment-oriented philosophies towards a restorative justice model, which focuses on restoring everyone involved to his or her precrime state. Restoration of the victim clearly is first priority. This idea is particularly well-suited to property crimes and, since nonviolent property crimes comprise about 40% of all juvenile crimes, restoring victims would greatly reduce the number of youths incarcerated, while at the same time providing victims with restitution for their losses.

With regard to juvenile crime, communities need to develop and support intensive early childhood intervention programs to promote healthy families. In most communities, schools are the focal point for youths and their families. Accordingly, schools need to be the focus for prevention programs. Since youths show maladaptive signals early in their lives, it is important to assure that intervention is provided in the early grades. Elementary schools need to focus on providing counselors and social service personnel, rather than metal detectors and armed police officers, to stop the violence.

There must be a continuum of sanctions available to local judges, permitting a disposition that will best meet the needs of the juvenile, victim, and community. This continuum should range from fines and community service sanctions to restoration of the victim, probation, in-home detention, and electronic monitoring. Incarceration should be the last resort, and incarceration of a juvenile in an adult facility must be an extremely rare occurrence.

Communities would be well-served to reduce the agency "turf" issues that keep well-coordinated services from families that are in need. In many communities, there is little or no coordination among welfare, juvenile court, state corrections, and law enforcement officials. These agencies have to staff the youth and family service needs together so that a realistic plan can be developed and implemented.

These recommendations are not expensive options when we compare the price to implement them with the costs necessary to fortify our schools and the $30–50,000 per year we spend to keep a child in an adult prison.

"Violent youth in adult court seem to be held more accountable."

Only the Most Violent Juvenile Criminals Should Be Tried in Adult Courts

Daniel L. Myers

In the following viewpoint Daniel L. Myers presents the results of a study of juvenile offenders in adult court. Violent juvenile criminals need to be punished severely, he asserts, and his study shows that this is best achieved through adult courts. While transferring less violent youth to these courts may be harmful, it is beneficial for violent offenders, maintains Myers, because adult courts ensure that juveniles are punished harshly for their crimes. Myers is an assistant professor of criminology at Indiana University of Pennsylvania, and conducts research on juvenile justice and delinquency.

As you read, consider the following questions:

1. Why do many commentators criticize adult court, according to Myers?
2. As argued by the author, what are the two perceived advantages of transferring juveniles to adult court?
3. What are the advantages of lengthier incarceration for violent offenders, in Myers's opinion?

Daniel L. Myers, "Adult Crime, Adult Time: Punishing Violent Youth in the Adult Criminal Justice System," *Youth Violence and Juvenile Justice*, vol. 1, April 2003, pp. 173–74, 176, 187–90. Copyright © 2003 by Sage Publications. Reproduced by permission.

During the past 30 years, there has been vigorous debate over the juvenile justice system's philosophy, structure, and procedures. Critical attacks have come from a variety of angles, focusing on such issues as insufficient enforcement of due process rights, inadequate treatment and rehabilitation services, abuse of the juvenile court's power, lenient treatment of offenders, and a general lack of direction in dealing with juvenile crime. These criticisms combined with rapid increases in violent juvenile arrest rates from the mid-1980s to the mid-1990s, a corresponding surge in firearm use among young people, and heavy media attention to adolescent offending have led to an erosion of the traditional juvenile court's philosophy and authority. In contrast to the conventional juvenile court's emphasis on "child saving" and serving the "best interests" of children, the "get-tough" philosophy, which originated in the adult criminal justice system during the 1970s, now extends into the juvenile system as well. A central issue is the transfer or waiver of juveniles to adult court, which often is described as a move toward "criminalizing" delinquent behavior.

An Increasing Desire for Harsh Punishment

Despite recent national decreases in violent juvenile arrest rates, youth violence continues to receive a considerable amount of public attention. . . . Many commentators have asserted that youthful offenders get off with a "slap on the wrist" in juvenile court, which in turn greatly contributes to overall levels of serious juvenile crime. In adult court, it is argued, a message can be sent that the lenient treatment of the juvenile system is no longer an option. Instead, harsh criminal court sanctions will be imposed, which will increase accountability and public safety while potentially decreasing motivations to commit future crimes.

All states have provisions that allow juveniles to be tried in adult court, and in modern times, few states have resisted the trend toward amending their juvenile codes to facilitate this process. Although almost all contemporary juvenile court judges retain the power to transfer certain cases, this authority also has been granted to some prosecutors, and legislatures have increasingly excluded certain types of offenses, offenders, or both from juvenile court jurisdiction. During the 1990s, these reforms resulted in increasing numbers of juveniles being sent to the adult system, particularly for violent offenses. Furthermore, efforts to increase the number of youth sent to adult court appear to be fueled by strong public support. Survey research in the past 10 years consistently shows a majority of the respondents favor trying juveniles in adult court for serious felonies, with roughly 75% of the typical adults surveyed believing that violent juvenile offenders should be treated as adults. . . .

The Punishment Process

Although many states have amended their juvenile statutes to include the elements of accountability, retribution, and enhanced public safety, it is not entirely clear that the adult criminal justice system can better serve these purposes when handling youthful offenders. A major expectation in transferring serious and violent juveniles to the adult system is that these youth will receive more certain and severe punishment than they otherwise would have received in juvenile court, and this increase in accountability and punishment will provide both general and specific deterrence, thereby reducing youthful offending. Unfortunately, although case outcomes of juveniles in adult court have been a major concentration in waiver research, the studies discussed next generally have been of uneven quality (many have been purely descriptive in nature, greatly limiting causal inference and the conclusions that can be made), and the findings from different pieces of research sometimes appear contradictory. . . .

A Study of Youth in Adult Court

The purpose of the current study was to provide a further examination of case processing outcomes for similar violent youth in juvenile and adult court. Using data from Pennsylvania, jurisdictional differences in punishment certainty, severity, and swiftness were investigated while controlling for a variety of legal and social factors that could impact on case outcomes. Specific consideration was given to the effect of the various independent variables on the likelihood of conviction and incarceration as well as on incarceration length and case processing time. . . .

In March 1996, legislation (known as *Act 33*) became effective in Pennsylvania that statutorily excludes certain violent youth from juvenile court jurisdiction. Pennsylvania's legislative waiver law targets two types of juveniles between the ages of 15 and 18: those who commit a violent felony offense with a deadly weapon and those who commit a violent felony offense after previously having been adjudicated delinquent on a violent felony offense. The current research examined offenders who were formally processed in Pennsylvania in 1994 and would have been excluded from juvenile court jurisdiction had the recent legislation been in effect at the time.

Specifically, data were analyzed pertaining to a cohort of 557 male juvenile offenders who were arrested for robbery, aggravated assault, or both and a deadly weapon was involved in their offense. These youth were between the ages of 15 and 18 at the time of the alleged act and received a juvenile court disposition sometime during 1994. Of the 557 offenders, 138 were transferred to adult criminal court by judicial waiver and 419 were retained in juvenile court. The essence of this study was to compare those juveniles transferred to adult court with those youth retained in juvenile court in terms of their case processing outcomes. . . .

Study Findings

In recent years, most states have moved to strengthen the sanctions available for responding to serious and violent youthful offending. Although a variety of get-tough mechanisms have been adopted, treating juvenile offenders as adults has been very popular. Proponents of transferring juveniles to adult court generally emphasize two perceived advantages with this approach: stronger punishment and greater public safety. Although the waived offenders in this study initially were more likely to be released from predispositional secure custody than were the youth retained in juvenile court, the subsequent treatment received by the offenders in adult court was consistently of a harsher nature. The transferred juveniles were more likely to be convicted, and of those who were convicted, youth in adult court were more likely to be convicted of a targeted offense of robbery or aggravated assault. Of the convicted offenders, those who were waived were also more likely to be incarcerated. Of those who were incarcerated, the transferred juveniles experienced longer periods of confinement. . . .

Violent Juvenile Crime: A Growing Problem

Growing numbers of young people, often from broken homes or so-called dysfunctional families, are committing murder, rape, robbery, kidnapping, and other violent acts. As [professor of politics and public affairs] John DiIulio and others argue, these emotionally damaged young people, growing up without faith, fathers, or families, often are the products of sexual or physical abuse. They live in an aimless and violent present; have no sense of the past and no hope for the future; and act, often ruthlessly, to gratify whatever urges or desires drive them at the moment. They commit unspeakably brutal crimes against other people, and their lack of remorse is shocking. They are what Professor DiIulio and others call urban "superpredators." They are the ultimate urban nightmare, and their numbers are growing. The number of juveniles arrested for violent crimes has increased nearly 60 percent over the last ten years [since 1992]. . . .

The juvenile justice system that prevails in many states today does juvenile criminals no favors by being lenient. According to a 1985 Rand Corporation study, "[w]aiting for chronic offenders to build a record of many arrests and minor dispositions only compounds the problems that must be dealt with later."

Since 1899, when Illinois adopted the first Juvenile Court Act, America's juvenile courts have been unable to deal effectively with the violent juvenile criminal. Law enforcement officers and a growing number of private citizens realize that this continuing failure undermines the credibility of the whole juvenile justice system.

The ultimate price for this failure, of course, is paid by innocent citizens.

James Wootten and Robert O. Heck, *Backgrounder*, October 28, 1996.

The results are fairly consistent with those of more recent research that has focused on violent youthful offenders and found that those in adult court experience higher conviction rates, greater incarceration rates, lengthier periods of confinement, and longer case processing times. The fact that violent youth can be and seemingly are punished more severely

in adult criminal court may be seen by some as enough reason to justify the expanded use of treating juveniles as adults.
With the continued popularity of the get-tough philosophy,
there is strong support for harsher sanctions, particularly if
they appear to increase community safety. Because violent
youth in adult court seem to be held more accountable and
are subjected to greater and lengthier incapacitation (including both incarceration and additional time on parole, which
can be revoked), politicians and the public alike may continue
to back transfer provisions. . . .

Adult Courts Are Effective for Violent Offenders

A . . . major issue concerns what should be done with juveniles who are to be housed in the adult criminal justice system. The main advantage that adult prisons appear to offer
over juvenile correctional facilities is the longer period of incarceration that can be provided. Lengthier incarceration not
only increases incapacitation, but it also has been found to be
associated with lesser recidivism on the part of serious and violent adolescent offenders. However, studies also suggest
that as compared to similar youth in juvenile institutions,
young offenders in adult prisons experience greater victimization by both inmates and staff, and receive inferior treatment services. In addition, a number of scholars have discussed the developmental differences between juveniles and
adults and have questioned the ability of the adult criminal
system to deal with immature and disadvantaged adolescents.
When these findings and arguments are considered along
with the previously mentioned findings of greater recidivism
among transferred youth, there is reason for caution in simply adopting an "adult crime, adult time" approach. . . .

In light of research findings and their own perceptions,
adult court judges may be reluctant to send all but the most
serious and violent youth to state prison. Instead, shorter
sentences may be imposed that allow the offender to remain
in a county facility. To the extent that this is true, the level of
educational and treatment services available to juveniles in
county jails and prisons could be cause for concern.

The results of this study and several others indicate that
violent juvenile offenders are punished more harshly in the

adult criminal justice system as compared to similar youth retained in juvenile court. However, other research findings and recent events (i.e., those in Pennsylvania) suggest reason for caution in adopting a widespread approach to waiving violent adolescents to adult court. Instead, more selective strategies seem warranted in which only the most violent youth (e.g., those employing firearms and chronic violent offenders) are targeted for criminal court processing. This appears to provide the best chance for accountability and punishment as well as for short- and long-term public safety.

"Adult criminal court is no place for a child. What works for adults does not work for children."

Juveniles Should Not Be Tried in Adult Courts

Malcom C. Young

Malcom C. Young maintains in the following viewpoint that children do not have the same understanding of the consequences of their actions as adults do, nor do they comprehend the nature of the criminal justice system. For these reasons, he argues, they are unable to defend themselves in an adult court. According to Young, many juveniles tried as adults are misunderstood and inappropriately sentenced. He believes that juveniles should remain in juvenile courts where they can receive age-appropriate treatment. Young is an attorney and executive director of The Sentencing Project, a Washington, D.C.–based organization that works to decrease the number of juveniles incarcerated in the United States.

As you read, consider the following questions:
1. Why do children love to talk to the police, in the author's opinion?
2. As explained by Young, why did people believe Nathaniel Brazill had no feelings?
3. According to the author, why do the laws of accountability not apply the same way to children?

Malcom C. Young, testimony before the Maryland State House Judiciary Committee, Annapolis, Maryland, March 6, 2003.

A number of my colleagues in the juvenile justice community who are here today [March 6, 2003] can well provide this [House Judiciary Committee] a deep understanding of the research and of what information that is known about children in the juvenile and criminal justice system. We share many of the same views on issues such as the hazards adult corrections pose for children, about racial disparity that shows up in the aggregate of decisions that send children to adult court, and about the developmental differences that distinguish children of different ages and leaves children ill-equipped to defend themselves in adult court.

Certainly this Committee does not need a reiteration of this information.

I also have another kind of experience that I offer the Committee.

Personal Experience

[In 1998], I was invited to join in the trial defense of a girl who was 13 at the time she was involved with an older male in a brutal homicide in Milwaukee, Wisconsin. I had not tried a case in nearly 20 years, but I agreed to do so after two meetings with the girl, which seemed to go well. Her name was Latasha Armstead.

Other cases followed. The case of a boy and his friend who simultaneously shot each other while playing a game together with the friend's father's guns. The boy took a bullet through his spinal cord just below his neck. During the first six hours of the paralysis which will be with him the rest of his life, he lay helplessly in blood on a bed next to his dying friend until the father came home and in horror called 911. The case of a boy called "J.P." in Missouri, who shot his favorite uncle in the back of the head with a 22-caliber rifle while the two of them were alone in the uncle's four-room frame house. "J.P." told so many different stories to the police that they charged him with murder. The sentencing of Nathaniel Brazill, who shot his favorite teacher in the front of his head and in front of a classroom of middle school students in West Palm Beach, Florida. And the case of a 15-year-old girl who allegedly hired a hit man to kill her boyfriend. After the hit man shot the boyfriend's brother from a car the girl was driving, she was charged with attempted murder. The case of a boy who in western Maryland stumbled stupidly into what ended up being charged as a carjacking. Most recently, I played a small part in the defense of one of the juveniles charged in the notorious beating death of a Milwaukee, Wisconsin man on a neighborhood porch one night last fall [2002]. . . .

Other attorneys have had more experience, but where I have been fortunate is in being given time to reflect upon what happened and what I saw in each of these cases. Thus, perhaps what I can offer this committee is the word of a person who has witnessed what it means for a child to be prosecuted in adult criminal court.

As a witness, I have drawn two conclusions about children in adult criminal court.

First, adult criminal court is *no place for a child*. What works for adults does not work for children. The child who finds himself or herself in adult court is penalized *in comparison to the adult* who has done something that is far worse. The irony is that transfer laws that put children into adult court were meant to punish them more severely than their peers who were left in juvenile court. Instead, children in adult court are penalized more severely than are adults in adult criminal court.

Second, *putting children in adult criminal court obscures or suppresses information that could be useful in preventing similar crimes or healing a community*. In the interest of future safety, we should see that this information comes out, and the way to do that is to retain more of these cases in juvenile court jurisdiction.

The Adult Criminal Court Is No Place for a Child

At age 15, Latasha Armstead testified in her defense at trial. I was the examining attorney. Question by question I took her through the events of the day of the murder of her grandmother's care nurse. I heard her speak clearly, with some force, and without much confusion. She sounded animated, she was on the stand for more than two hours, she did not collapse, she provided detail and sequence. She admitted to certain acts and denied others. I was elated. It had taken many hours to prepare and I went home at the end of the day feeling it had been well worth it.

The next day's newspaper was a cold splash in the face. The reporter described Latasha speaking in a "flat monotone," and that she "showed no emotion as she recounted [the victim's] slaying." The report bode ill for the jury.

What the reporter or the jury didn't know was that Latasha spoke longer and in more detail, and with greater emphasis in court than she had ever spoken at any time about the homicide. Sometimes, in the juvenile lock-up, she would refuse to speak at all. Or, she would change the subject or put her head on the table. For many days she was as flat in affect as could be. Yet when the nice young lay pastor from a local church walked into the room, she became animated, open, laughing. Not so with us. I would talk with her for hours, plying out questions, and then come back, just to hear her tell her story once.

Because I had seen how she could close down, for me, her direct testimony in court was a major success. Latasha had come so far, tried so hard, and she did indeed feel pain. We felt it next to her at the counsel table. For the jury, though, she didn't work well. Shellow, the attorney experienced with children, told me this happens all the time. Cross examination was another nightmare. Mark Williams, a seasoned prosecutor, didn't raise his voice or shout or yell. He was simply "nice" and "gentle" with Latasha. She wanted to please him, and wanted to believe that a man who was nice would not hurt her. But he led her into simply denying any memory of giving statements to the police. As a result, she could not explain to the jury as she had many times to us that the police had led her into saying that she had "planned" the crime with her boyfriend and that she "knew" there would be a crime of some sort. We believed that these were their words, not hers. Our belief was of little use. The prosecution would use those words in evidence in the police reports to make their case that this 13-year-old girl had the degree of intent required to convict her of murder.

And the fact was, the prosecutor had police reports with Latasha's statements plastered all over them. Children love to talk to police. They feel protected. After all, kids are told that if they get lost, the only person to talk to is a police officer, that a police officer will help them. But after they have answered questions, and the police have written down what they say, children quickly forget what they said. If the police talk to them a second time, there will be a second, different story. The police write that story down as well. Now with multiple statements in the police reports, there are "impeaching" statements that prosecutors will use to "prove" that the child was lying. . . .

Misunderstood

In part of her testimony Latasha was to use a diagram representing the face and neck of the woman who was killed to demonstrate her actions. In hours of preparation, we were not able to get her to use this graphic aid for the jury. She lacked the adult experience in interpreting abstract or representative drawings. The judge denied our use of the diagrams, so we were spared the possibility that Latasha would simply freeze up when presented with them. When adults testify, the witness stand is a fairly powerful revelation of character. When children testify, the witness stand is a place where truth is concealed or distorted. Nathaniel Brazill testified in his own defense at his trial; a month later when we arrived in West Palm Beach people who saw him on television were still talking about how cold and calculating he appeared. We heard time and again: "The boy has no feelings!"

A week after we started working with Nathaniel, the reason for his cool appearance became quite clear. The boy suffered some kind of learning or communication disability (which was actually diagnosed for the first time in the jail). To compensate it seems that he had learned to politely ask to have a question repeated while he "processed" what was asked of him the first time. His reply would be deliberate, slow. Teachers loved his demeanor. To them he seemed to be a learner, and respectful. Actually he was having a hard time grasping what was going on around him. In any case, the pattern of behavior that favorably impressed teachers looked absolutely terrible in a child who is on the witness stand. . . .

Still Just a Child

Sitting next to a child on trial in an adult courtroom provides a score of reminders that, regardless of what the child was involved in, he or she is still just a child. Defendants are supposed to elect whether they want a jury or a judge trial, a serious decision that requires weighing many factors. A child will decide on the basis of the fiction that "the judge likes me," or doesn't, as the case may be.

Rehabilitation

The juvenile justice system is supposed to concentrate on reforming youthful offenders, not letting them rot behind bars—a sensible approach, since they are unformed and far more susceptible to change than veteran adult criminals. Rehabilitation also recognizes the obvious: Children are less blameworthy than adults because, through no fault of their own, they lack the maturity and self-control that we expect of their elders. Giving up on a 14-year-old may sound like tough-minded realism, but it's really irresponsible defeatism.

Steve Chapman, *Conservative Chronicle*, August 17, 2003.

A child will be more interested in whether a former boyfriend will say, if called to testify, that he still loves her, than if the boyfriend will claim he heard her threaten to kill him.

Although defendants are supposed to assist and advise their lawyers in the selection of a jury, a child will decide on the basis of the color of a dress or because a juror looks like Uncle Fred.

And in Latasha's case, the most important question in her mind was whether her mother had come to court. "No," her attorneys had to say, "the mother who abandoned you for the streets and never visited you in detention isn't going to be here, and now please listen to the police officer's testimony so you can help us ask questions." But the child isn't listening. She continues to mourn after her missing mother as the trial swirls on around her.

In adult court, the important questions are not asked or answered, and the lessons about how to reduce juvenile crime are lost. . . .

Children Do Not Understand Consequences

Criminal law and court trials are rooted in the hypothesis that one can be presumed to be responsible for the logical consequences of his or her actions. The laws of accountability, the instructions given a jury that is to decide the level of intent or state of mind of the defendant, are all based on this premise. This hypothesis works, more or less, for adults. The task for the prosecutor at trial is to show where the defendant was and what the defendant did leading up to the crime. The task for the defense is to either show that the defendant wasn't there or didn't do it, or that what he did was different, from what the prosecutor attempts to show.

For adults, this is often enough.

But children cannot be said to understand as well the consequences of their acts. That is why we have signs that warn drivers against "children playing." A child will dart into the street, an adult is expected not to do so. When children do dramatic or surprising things, we know we have to plumb their background and experience to understand why. We thought that Latasha Armstead's background, which included being raped multiple times at a very young age, being abandoned by her mother, and then taking care of by an elderly and bed-ridden grandmother, might have had something to do with her attachment to the older boy who actually took the life of the victim and Latasha's ability to make a decision about what she should have done. Under the trial judge's application of rules of evidence, very little of that background information came before the jury. The trial focused on the immediate actions, not the background of the girl. In Nathaniel Brazill's case, the prosecution seems to have built its case around the presumption that a person who goes into a school, points a gun at someone and pulls the trigger intends to kill that person. This is logical for an adult. The trial defense attempted to counter this with an image of Nathaniel Brazill as a model student from a good family home. The jury convicted Nathaniel of a lesser included offense to First Degree Murder, so the defense strategy was partly successful.

Background Is Important

However, the trial defense unintentionally obscured the fact that Nathaniel Brazill's academic performance was dropping dramatically, and that he came from a home where he had witnessed violence and domestic discord, lived in fear of his mother's death from cancer, and where alcohol was a family weakness. All these things were contrary to the image of the defendant that the attorneys were trying to project, so they avoided them.

Similarly, the girl who was charged with hiring a hit man to kill her boyfriend went to trial portrayed as a "good" girl who got in with the wrong crowd. The opposite was true: she had been involved in sex and drugs without her parents' knowledge for several years, was highly dependent, capable of a high degree of fantasy and drama which she could put in motion without any apparent sense of what might transpire as a result. Typically she was more interested in preserving her parents' image of her as "good" than in raising a strong defense to a serious criminal charge.

Juveniles Should Stay in Juvenile Court

Should anyone care that criminal trials seem to be such poor vehicles for revealing the backgrounds and histories that might help explain serious, violent acts by juveniles? In my opinion, our best hope for curbing violence and serious crime, and probably a lot of the less serious crime among children, lies in learning more about why children do bad things in the first place. I suppose, if another person believes that tough adult sentences to decades in prison will do more to reduce crime, the nuances of a criminal court trial are of little interest, and it matters not if we continue to bury or conceal the information that explains what goes on in the lives of children involved in serious crime.

But one can have doubts about the utility of tough adult sentences alone. . . .

Unless there is a judicial determination, children's cases should stay in juvenile court. It is the right place for a child to be. It is the court that is better suited to answer the questions we really need to know if we are to reduce or prevent serious juvenile crime.

Periodical Bibliography

The following articles have been selected to supplement the diverse views presented in this chapter.

Terrie Albano	"Juvenile Justice Is Elusive," *People's Weekly World*, March 17, 2001.
Michael D. Bradbury	"More Tools Are Needed to Curb Juvenile Violence," *Los Angeles Times*, February 29, 2000.
Judith Browne	"Schoolhouse to Jailhouse: We're Too Eager to Lock Up Kids," *Progressive Populist*, September 15, 2003.
Steve Chapman	"Juvenile Murders and Other Crimes," *Conservative Chronicle*, August 17, 2003.
Lili Frank Garfinkel and Renelle Nelson	"Promoting Better Interaction Between Juvenile Court, Schools, and Parents," *Reclaiming Children and Youth*, Spring 2004.
Jennifer Gonnerman	"Kids on the Row," *Village Voice*, January 11, 2000.
Sue Gunawardena-Vaughn	"Juvenile Executions a 'Shameful Practice,'" *People's Weekly World*, November 16, 2002.
Mirah A. Horowitz	"Kids Who Kill: A Critique of How the American Legal System Deals with Juveniles Who Commit Homicide," *Law and Contemporary Problems*, Summer 2000.
Arianna Huffington	"Activists Turn the Tide Against More Jails for Juveniles," *Los Angeles Times*, July 29, 2001.
Arianna Huffington	"Second Chance for Youth May Be Endangered Species," *Los Angeles Times*, February 29, 2000.
Adam Liptak	"Juvenile Executions," *New York Times*, September 1, 2002.
Patrick T. Murphy	"Convicted at 14," *New York Times*, May 17, 2001.
Sara Rimer	"Man Who Killed at 17 Is Scheduled to Die," *New York Times*, May 27, 2002.
Connie de la Vega	"Going It Alone: The Rest of the Civilized World Has Abolished the Death Penalty. Will the United States Follow Suit?" *American Prospect*, July 2004.

CHAPTER 3

How Can Juvenile Crime and Violence Be Prevented?

Chapter Preface

In 1978 seventeen teenagers—convicted of crimes such as assault and battery, arson, burglary, and vandalism—were taken for a visit inside Rabway, a maximum-security prison in New Jersey. In an attempt to convince the youth to give up crime, prison guards and inmates there tried to scare them straight by giving them a realistic and shocking account of the brutality of life in prison. The youth were threatened and intimidated, and received explicit descriptions of sex and violence in the prison. Since the 1960s, juvenile courts and prisons have been conducting "scared straight" programs such as this in an attempt to deter juvenile crime. However, like many proposals to prevent juvenile crime, these programs have been controversial. While advocates maintain that they prevent juvenile crime, many critics argue that scared straight programs do not work, and may actually increase the risk of juvenile crime.

Many of these programs' most vocal proponents are youth who have participated in them. Kandice—a teenager who ran away from home at age thirteen, became a prostitute, and tried to kill herself—argues for the effectiveness of scared straight programs. When a judge sent Kandice to spend time in prison with two former prostitutes, she saw the frightening reality of life as a prostitute, and immediately turned her life around. "[My life changed] as soon as I got home," she says. "I started studying, stopped ditching, and became an honor student. Because of scared straight," says Kandice, "I'm alive today."

However, opponents of scared straight programs argue that while there are success stories like Kandice's, for the majority of teenagers these programs actually cause an increase in crime. According to a report in the *Harvard Mental Health Letter*, in one study of scared straight programs, more than 40 percent of the participants committed new offenses during the six months following their completion of the program, compared with only 10 percent of youth who did not participate. The researchers conclude that, "During prison visits, [youth] may be responding not to the explicit preaching of adult inmates but to the underlying suggestion that a criminal life is thrilling. The adults become models rather than bad examples."

Because juvenile crime continues to be a problem, debates over how best to prevent it will likely continue. In addition to scared straight programs, many other approaches have been tried, such as harsh punishments and school security measures. The authors in the following chapter offer various opinions on this controversial topic.

> "*Society's failure to take punitive action in dealing with first-time youthful offenders is a primary factor contributing to the development of habitual criminals.*"

Harsh Punishment Is the Best Way to Prevent Juvenile Crime

Kenneth W. Sukhia

Juvenile crime is a serious problem, contends Kenneth W. Sukhia in the following viewpoint, and has been made even worse by the juvenile justice system's failure to effectively punish young offenders. In Sukhia's opinion, the best way to fight juvenile crime is to implement swift and certain punishments. Young criminals who are not harshly punished are likely to commit further and more serious crimes, he maintains. Sukhia is a lawyer with the Fowler White Boggs Banker law firm in Florida. He formerly served as the U.S. attorney for that state.

As you read, consider the following questions:

1. According to Eugene Methvin, how many contacts with the criminal justice system does a youngster usually have prior to receiving any formal charges from a judge?
2. At what age are criminals most violent and prolific, according to Harry Shorstein?
3. In the author's opinion, why is it important to punish small, "quality of life" offenses?

Kenneth W. Sukhia, testimony before the U.S. House Subcommittee on Crime, Committee on the Judiciary, Washington, DC, March 10, 1999.

D espite recent positive trends, our nation continues to record one of the highest violent crime rates in the world. Since 1960, the population of the United States has increased some 43%, yet the number of violent crimes has increased over 500%. While violent crime is a rarity in some countries, in America someone falls prey to a crime of violence every 17 seconds and one of us is murdered every 25 minutes.

No small contributor to this epidemic has been the astounding increase in juvenile crime. . . .

The tragic toll across our nation is measured not only in numbers, but in human pain. In Arkansas, three eight-year-olds are raped and murdered, allegedly by three teenage boys participating in a satanic ritual. In Texas, six teenagers are accused of mindlessly raping and strangling two young girls who stumbled onto a drug gang's initiation rite. In Florida, four youths are involved in the brutal and senseless murder of a British tourist at an interstate rest stop in a small rural community. . . .

Results of an Ineffective Juvenile Justice System

I have seen firsthand the devastating effects of an ineffective juvenile justice system. One of the last cases I prosecuted as United States Attorney was a carjacking case out of Gainesville, Florida. Five persons, including one 19-year-old, two 18-year-olds and two 14-year-olds, shot a 72-year-old man in Ocala and later abducted a 19-year-old college student in Gainesville. As it turned out, the defendants collectively had numerous prior juvenile arrests for such offenses as attempted first degree murder, aggravated assault, and assault and battery, and one of the juveniles had dozens of prior auto theft arrests in his background. Despite these arrests, the juvenile displayed a defiant attitude, telling me that he had never served a day in jail and that "you can't touch me." Two years before he committed the carjacking in our case, and while he was a juvenile, one of the 18-year-olds in the group participated in a drive-by shooting. When he was 16, the 19-year-old triggerman in the group brandished a firearm, pulled a lady from her car, yanked the purse from her shoulder and drove off in her vehicle. Remarkably, after being convicted in the Florida system for that offense, the man served only four months and was released. Thankfully, in his first experience with the federal system he was convicted after jury trial and sentenced to 20 years in federal prison with no parole in our carjacking case. Ironically, even though we were the federal prosecutors in the case, we only learned of the prior juvenile offenses because we were working closely with the State Attorney to pursue the juveniles through the state system.

Not surprisingly, the juveniles responsible for the murder of the British tourist referred to above also had extensive prior arrests in the juvenile system without having been subjected to any meaningful punishment in the past. Two of the boys were 16 and the other two were 13 and 14. They were charged with first degree murder, attempted first degree murder, and auto theft. According to newspaper accounts at the time, the 13-year-old arrested for the crime had a record of 15 arrests on more than 50 charges. The local School Superintendent commented that "some of these kids have arrest records you wouldn't believe."

Swift and Certain Punishment

As discussed by [researcher] Eugene Methvin in the Summer of 1997 issue of *Policy Review*, studies at the University of Southern California and by criminologist Marvin Wolfgang in Philadelphia, revealed that swift and certain punishment for convicted felons in the early stages of their criminal activity is a most effective means of suppressing crime.

In his *Policy Review* article, Methvin cited numerous studies confirming that society's failure to take punitive action in dealing with first-time youthful offenders is a primary factor contributing to the development of habitual criminals. As Mr. Methvin noted, "a troublesome youngster typically has ten or 12 contacts with the criminal-justice system and many more undiscovered offenses before he ever receives any formal 'adjudication,' or finding of guilt, from a judge. He quickly concludes that he will never face any serious consequences for his delinquency." Our experience in Florida clearly bears this out.

State Attorney Harry Shorstein from Duval County has consistently advocated and implemented a strategy of early intervention with punishments of graduated severity for youthful offenders. Mr. Shorstein notes that "it is from age 11 to age 18 that criminals are the most violent and most prolific . . . yet, almost all of our crime-fighting money at every level of government goes to fighting crimes" perpetrated by adult offenders. Accordingly to Mr. Shorstein, "that's the biggest mistake we're committing" in the criminal justice system today. "The worst thing we can do is try a juvenile as an adult and then put him or her on probation," says Shorstein. "It reinforces the failures of the existing criminal justice juvenile system, which has never given good judges the means with which to punish serious juvenile behavior." Based on his extensive experience in the state criminal justice system, Mr. Shorstein concludes that meaningful punishment for early offenders, including incarceration where appropriate during a person's "most prolific and violent period" will "probably prevent more crime than . . . the lifetime incarceration of a 25-year-old."

As reported recently in newspapers across the state, last year [1998] alone Florida poured $512 million into youth "programs that provide counseling, education and lessons on behavior," with "little to show for it." No social program can undo the devastating effect of a youthful criminal's exposure to a juvenile justice system which allows repeated criminal conduct to go unpunished. As the studies cited by Eugene Methvin confirm, the state's failure to take punitive action in dealing with first-time youthful offenders is a primary factor contributing to the development of habitual criminals.

Recommendations for Improving the Situation

1. Long Term.

Given the disparity between the number of violent crimes committed by juveniles and the number of facilities available to detain them over the last decade . . . , juvenile offenders have been taught to believe through repeated brushes with the system that unless they commit murder, they stand little or no chance of being incarcerated for their crimes. It seems obvious that until juvenile offenders who commit violent crimes understand that they will be punished for their crimes, there will continue to be no meaningful deterrent to juvenile crime in Florida and elsewhere in our nation. Putting violent and chronic juvenile offenders into an adult system which itself does not deal effectively with violent crime is no meaningful solution. This sentiment is echoed by officials with the Florida Department of Juvenile Justice who believe our state would greater benefit from enhanced juvenile justice programs outside the adult system, as long as our judges remain reluctant to impose meaningful punishment through the adult system on juvenile offenders.

Violent and Property Crime Committed by Juveniles

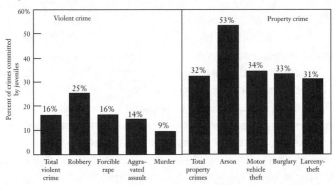

In 2000, 16% of all violent crimes (robbery, forcible rape, aggravated assault and murder) and 32% of all property crimes (arson, motor vehicle theft, burglary and larceny-theft) were committed by people under the age of 18. Of those crimes, the most common one committed by juveniles was arson; 53% of all arson crimes were committed by young people.

Office of Juvenile Justice and Deliquency Prevention, 2002.

The long-term solution to the problem of juvenile crime clearly falls largely outside the law enforcement system. It requires strengthening of the basic institutions of family, schools, religious organizations and community groups which are responsible for instilling values and helping to raise law-abiding citizens. From a law enforcement perspective, however, there can be no meaningful deterrent to ongoing juvenile crime as long as juvenile offenders believe they will never be subjected to meaningful punishment for their crimes.

2. Build More Youth Detention Facilities.

Accordingly, we must commit to the building of a sufficient number of youth detention facilities to provide an adequate deterrent to those who would commit crime.

3. To Protect the Innocent, Violent Juvenile Offenders Must Be Punished and Removed from Society.

We must insure that violent and hardened juvenile offenders, who are responsible for a large share of the violent crime increase in Florida and our nation, are removed from society and punished. Increasingly, these violent criminals are being transferred to the adult system which seems incapable of imposing adequate punishment, and which fails to incarcerate 85 percent of the juveniles certified for adult treatment. . . .

We Must Recognize That Juvenile Crime Is Never "Small"

Punishing juveniles for engaging in "quality of life" offenses such as under-age drinking, urinating in the street, jumping turnstiles at public transit facilities and painting graffiti on public and private property renders significant results toward eliminating more serious crimes. During 1994, Mayor Rudolph Giuliani and his appointed Police Commissioner, William Bratton, instituted a program to eliminate the quality-of-life offenses which pervaded the streets and subways of New York. Giuliani and Bratton placed both uniformed and undercover officers throughout the City's subway system and other key juvenile crime areas arresting fare evaders, graffiti vandals and other "quality of life" offenders. When violators were arrested or detained for these type offenses, they were often found in possession of stolen weapons or other items. Moreover, during questioning they provided information about other offenses and perpetrators, resulting in arrests of violent and habitual criminals.

According to Jeffrey Fagan, Director of Columbia University's Center for Violent Research and Prevention, Mayor Giuliani's and Commissioner Bratton's efforts put in motion a crime fighting strategy which has yielded phenomenal results. For example, New York City's murders declined by 49%, robberies by 43% and burglaries by 39%. In 1995, the City accounted for 70% of the national decline in serious crimes. Juvenile "quality of life" offenders were sent a message that their lawlessness would no longer be ignored, but rather result in certain and swift punishment.

Whatever else can be said about the juvenile crime issue, it is clear that with Florida's current juvenile crime levels and with a dramatic increase in juvenile population anticipated during the next 15 years, we have no choice but to take strong and immediate steps to address the issue. A weak and indulgent response to juvenile crime serves an injustice to both the society which suffers from the effects of such crime and to the juvenile offender who is encouraged through repeated conduct which goes unpunished to escalate his criminal activity. To fail to act responsibly to address this crucial problem is to disserve both the law-abiding public and our state's youthful offenders.

*"There is no scientific research indicating
. . . that punitive strategies have a general
deterrent effect on [juvenile crime]."*

Harsh Punishment Is Not the Best Way to Prevent Juvenile Crime

Laura H. Carnell

In the following viewpoint Laura H. Carnell argues that while harshly punishing juvenile offenders may sometimes be effective, in most situations young criminals will be better deterred from crime by treatment and rehabilitation programs outside the court system. For the majority of young offenders, harsh punishments may actually increase the chance of future criminal activity, maintains Carnell. She advocates an individualized assessment approach to juvenile crime, where punishment is tailored to the individual offender. Carnell is a professor of psychology at Temple University in Philadelphia, and director of the John D. and Catherine T. MacArthur Foundation Research Network on Adolescent Development and Juvenile Justice.

As you read, consider the following questions:
1. What is the best and least-costly response to most first-time offenders, according to the author?
2. In Carnell's opinion, what is the danger of interrupting a young person's educational or occupational development by sending him or her to prison?
3. According to the author, why will forcing states to implement mandatory sentencing programs be harmful to the juvenile justice system?

Laura H. Carnell, testimony before the U.S. House Subcommittee on Crime, Committee on the Judiciary, Washington, DC, March 11, 1999.

I can think of very few topics that inspire more heated, or more misinformed, debate than that of juvenile crime. I would like to take this opportunity, as a social scientist who works with hard facts, and not inflamed rhetoric, to clarify a number of key issues. . . .

Individualized Punishment

If there is one thing that research on effective responses to juvenile offending tells us, it is that there is no such thing as "one size fits all," even when we are talking about youngsters who have committed the very same offense. I agree that we should respond with celerity and certainty to all juvenile offenses, no matter how minor. But the best response—the one that is most likely to prevent future offending—depends on the offender and the circumstances of the offense. More than two-thirds of nonviolent offenders never reoffend at all, without any sanction or intervention whatsoever. For most first-time offenders, therefore, diversion out of the justice system is the best and least-costly response, and the response that has the least likelihood of harming that child's life in a way that will have long-term repercussions. Other juveniles may need some sort of intensive intervention, either family-based or through a supervised community-based program. A smaller number will require some sort of longer-term residential placement. Some need treatment for substance abuse, while others need special education, and still others need psychological counseling. Some may need all of the above. Adolescence is a time of tremendous variability.

I am not opposed to sanctions for juvenile offenders. Indeed, there are some offenders for whom punishment is a very appropriate response. But there are other offenders who will be affected by the very same punishment in a way that will make them more likely, not less likely, to reoffend. We know that this is especially likely if the punishment brings the nonviolent offender into contact with violent and more serious delinquents, or with adult criminals. Adolescence is a critical period in development, a period during which many decisions and choices have long-term implications for the successful transition into adulthood. A young person whose educational or occupational development is interrupted when it need not be—for instance, if a juvenile who actually is not dangerous is forced to spend time in a correctional institution—will end up at greater risk for later unemployment, mental health problems, and criminal activity. Surely none of us here wishes to respond to a juvenile offender in a way that is going to increase that juvenile's chances of becoming a danger to the community.

My point is that effective intervention requires the careful, individualized assessment of a juvenile's history and living circumstances, as well as the conditions surrounding the offense. I am concerned that any prescribed system of mandatory, graduated sanctions that is based solely on the nature and number of a juvenile's offenses, without taking into account the juvenile's history and stage of development, will impede the justice system's ability to respond intelligently and with appropriate flexibility. Moreover, the system's ability to respond effectively will be further compromised by implementing policies that will mandate that we process proportionately more nonviolent offenders through court, the majority of whom could be safely diverted from the system, at tremendous savings to taxpayers.

[Congressional hearings about juvenile crime] rarely include testimony about the juvenile justice system's successes—young people who, through appropriate diversion or effective rehabilitation, return to their community and develop into productive, taxpaying citizens. Of course it is possible to recount stories of offenders who were not sanctioned initially and who later reoffended, perhaps even violently. But this is not evidence that the reoffending would not have occurred if these juveniles who *were* sanctioned, even harshly, and who, after their release, went on to reoffend—as research on youngsters who have been tried and incarcerated as adults indicates. As some of you know, reoffending is more likely among juveniles who have been sanctioned within the criminal justice system than it is among their counterparts who have been sanctioned and treated as juveniles.

Harsher Punishments Are Not Always Better

It is tempting to think that if a given punishment has not worked, the sensible thing to do is to punish the person more, or more harshly. But more is not always better. When a drug that has been prescribed for an illness fails to work, the best response is not always to give more of the same medicine. Indeed, quite often the best response is to change the course of treatment entirely. In the case of a juvenile who has offended more than once, the best response is to examine what was done initially, figure out why it was not effective, and respond in a way that is likely to be successful. We can easily make things worse by intervening in a way that is inappropriate for a given offender.

The Importance of Parental Involvement

Most advocates believe that the juvenile justice system needs more involvement from parents in order to serve the best interests of the child. . . . Most professionals in juvenile court recognize that parents, parent surrogates, and others who may be important in a youth's life should have the opportunity to be involved in the court process and any out-of-home placement. . . .

Parents have greater knowledge about their child than anyone else. They understand their child's disability needs and what approaches have been successful at school and at home. They may understand which medications have been effective and which have produced problematic side effects. They have learned their child's individual learning style. . . . Most importantly, they want to be involved and can provide information to the court which will assist their child.

Lili Frank and Renelle Nelson, *Reclaiming Children and Youth*, Spring 2004.

There is no scientific research indicating that increasing the severity of a juvenile's punishment lessens the chance of his or her reoffending, and there is even some evidence that severe sanctions actually *increase* the risk of reoffending. Nor is there any evidence that punitive strategies have a general deterrent effect on juveniles. In contrast, there is strong research showing that high-quality, developmentally-appropriate, adequately-funded, delinquency prevention and treatment programs work. States and local communities need the funding and freedom to develop and maintain effective prevention programs, high-quality comprehensive interventions for serious juvenile offenders, and secure residential facilities for the small proportion of offenders who pose a genuine risk to public safety.

Mandatory Sanctions Will Not Work

The general principle of responding differently to repeat offenders than first offenders is a reasonable one, and one with which I concur. But insisting that all juvenile offenders be sanctioned punitively, and mandating that the severity of the punishment must increase with each offense in a rigid, predetermined fashion is both unwise and potentially dangerous. Forcing states to implement a mandatory graduated sanctions policy for nonviolent offenders will siphon money away from delinquency prevention and treatment programs that work. It will overburden an already overwhelmed and inadequately funded juvenile justice system. And it is likely to have the unintentional effect of increasing, not decreasing, violent juvenile offending.

Changes in juvenile justice policy need to be based on solid research evidence, not intuition or anecdote. In this case, the research evidence points conclusively to the benefits of individualized, developmentally-appropriate responses to juvenile offending. In order to promote public safety, Congress should support state and local initiatives to do just this.

"Citizens with guns helped stop about a third of the post-1997 public school shootings, stepping in before uniformed police could arrive."

Teachers Should Be Armed to Prevent School Violence

John R. Lott Jr.

Banning guns in school is not the best way to prevent school violence, contends John R. Lott Jr. in the following viewpoint. He argues instead that allowing teachers to be armed is the most effective deterrent of violence. In addition, Lott maintains, by allowing teachers to carry guns, any attacks that do occur will be stopped more quickly. Lott is a resident scholar at the American Enterprise Institute for Public Policy Research, and author of *The Bias Against Guns.*

As you read, consider the following questions:
1. According to Lott, where do multiple-victim shootings in the United States most commonly take place?
2. How many times each year do Americans use guns defensively, according to the author?
3. What do annual surveys of crime victims in the United States show, as cited by Lott?

B anning guns from schools seems the obvious way to keep children safe. Utah, though, is doing the opposite, and is stirring up debate across the nation.

Acting under a new state law, school districts across Utah have started drawing up regulations allowing teachers and other public employees to carry concealed guns on school property.[1] Opponents are still trying to fight the law, and at first glance their concern about firearms in schools is understandable. Last Sunday [July 6, 2003] in New Jersey, an attack by armed teenagers against three fellow students and randomly chosen townspeople was narrowly averted.

Deterring Criminals

But that's not the whole picture. Consider an analogy: Suppose a criminal is stalking you or your family. Would you feel safe putting a sign in front of your home saying, "This Home Is a Gun-Free Zone"? Law-abiding citizens might be pleased by such a sign, but to criminals it would be an invitation.

In 1985, just eight states had right-to-carry laws—laws that automatically grant permits for concealed weapons once applicants pass a criminal background check, pay their fees and, when required, complete a training class. Today [2003], 35 states do.

Examining all the multiple-victim public shootings in the United States from 1977 to 1999 shows that on average, states that adopt right-to-carry laws experience a 60% drop in the rates at which the attacks occur, and a 78% drop in the rates at which people are killed or injured from such attacks.

To the extent such attacks still occurred in right-to-carry states, they overwhelmingly take place in so-called "gun-free zones." Indeed, the attack last week in Meridian, Miss., in which five people were killed took place in a Lockheed Martin plant where employees were forbidden to have guns.

The effect of right-to-carry laws is greater on multiple-victim public shootings than on other crimes for a simple reason: Increasing the probability that someone will be able to protect himself improves deterrence. Though it may be

---

1. In March 2003 Utah passed a law that gives licensed handgun owners the right to carry their weapons into any Utah school.

statistically unlikely that any single person in a crowd is carrying a concealed handgun, the probability that at least one person is armed is high.

Citizens with Guns Can Stop Crime

Contrary to many people's impressions, before the federal law was enacted in 1995 [prohibiting guns in schools] it was possible for teachers and other adults with concealed-handgun permits to carry guns on school property in many states.

Many of the concerns about accidents and other problems are unwarranted. The real problems at schools occurred only after the ban. The rash of student shootings at schools began in October 1997 in Pearl, Miss.

Schools Are Defenseless

Any monster who chooses to ignore the laws and commit murder at random knows he will find no opposition on school grounds, until police arrive.

The "gun control" crowd likes to refer to schools as "safe zones." In reality, they're "defenseless zones." The "gun control" crowd has made sure no responsible adult civilian could defend the innocents at Columbine High School in Littleton [Colorado, where twelve students were shot and killed in 1999].

Ralph D. Sherman, *Hartford Courant*, April 30, 1999.

Public reaction against guns is understandable, given the horrific events shown on TV. But the more than 2 million times each year that Americans use guns defensively are never discussed. In more than 90% of those cases, simply brandishing a weapon is sufficient to cause a criminal to break off an attack. My research also shows that citizens with guns helped stop about a third of the post-1997 public school shootings, stepping in before uniformed police could arrive.

Last year [2002], news broadcasts on the three main TV networks carried about 190,000 words on gun crime stories. Not one segment featured a civilian using a gun to stop a crime. Newspapers are not much better.

Police are extremely important in deterring crime, but they almost always arrive after the crime has been committed. Annual surveys of crime victims in the United States by the Justice Department show that when confronted by a criminal, people are safest if they have a gun.

Just as the threat of arrest and prison can deter criminals, so can the fact that victims can defend themselves.

For multiple-victim shootings, the biggest factor determining the amount of harm is the length of time between when an attack starts and when someone with a gun can stop the attack. The longer the delay, the more are harmed.

Good intentions do not necessarily make good laws. What counts is whether the laws ultimately save lives. Unfortunately, too many gun laws disarm law-abiding citizens, not criminals.

"I have a problem with the presumption that all gun owners are responsible, respectful, disciplined people, even if they have no criminal records."

Arming Teachers Is Not an Effective Way to Prevent School Violence

Jacquelyn Mitchard

Allowing teachers to carry guns in schools will not make children safer, maintains Jacquelyn Mitchard in the following viewpoint. She argues that arming teachers would create a number of serious safety risks; for example, a teacher might lose patience with students and threaten them with a gun, or a teacher's gun might be misplaced and found by children. Finally, says Mitchard, arming teachers will damage the trusting relationship that many students have with their teachers. Mitchard writes a weekly column about topics that affect the family for the *Milwaukee Journal Sentinel*, and is the author of *A Theory of Relativity*.

As you read, consider the following questions:
1. For what age children is gun violence a significant cause of death, as cited by the author?
2. What example does Mitchard give to illustrate her belief that not all teachers can be trusted to look after their students responsibly?
3. In the author's opinion, why is school the only place that some children feel safe?

Jacquelyn Mitchard, "What's the Lesson If Teachers Pack Heat?" *Milwaukee Journal Sentinel*, November 9, 2003. Copyright © 2003 by the *Milwaukee Journal Sentinel*. Reproduced by permission of the author.

With 35 states allowing citizens without criminal records to carry concealed weapons, why does it bother me that kindergarten teachers may soon be able to pack a shooting iron along with their colored pencils and alphabet cards?

The high court in Utah, the state that brought back that grand old tradition—capital punishment—is leading the way, by removing the ban on carrying concealed weapons on university campuses.[1] According to writer John Lott Jr., whose lifework is ridding our society of the cancer of the bias against firearms, it's about time that schools be safe places to learn and play—and guns can make them that way again.

Maybe he's right.

Lott's Argument

Why would it matter, given that many high schools now routinely employ armed police officers to guard against mayhem, if it were your child's algebra instructor who had a nice .22 Ruger [gun]?

After all, though the American Association of Pediatrics is of the opinion that no household where children live should contain guns or ammunition, nobody said anything about school.

Lott bemoans the unfairness of namby-pamby media types who forget that Americans use guns more than 2 million times a year in self-defense. They're too busy concentrating on the fact that gun violence is a significant cause of death for children ages 15 to 19.

In fact, Lott, and others like him, don't consider youths over the age of 15 "children."

He gets really torqued when a sub-adult (especially, although this is never specified, a member of the underclass) is thrown into the same category as an actual child—although he had no problem writing about "students" who prevented a school massacre by fetching their guns, even though these were criminal-justice students, some ages 25 or older.

After all, gun-toting teachers, and even gun-toting stu-

1. In March 2003 Utah passed a law that gives licensed handgun owners the right to carry their weapons into any Utah school.

dents, could make schools a safer place—for the people with the guns, at least.

Can Teachers Be Trusted with Guns?

And yet, I have a problem with the presumption that all gun owners are responsible, respectful, disciplined people, even if they have no criminal records.

While we entrust our children's psychological well-being to teachers every day, they are no more or less likely to snap their caps—especially in a stressful environment; and kids, judging only by my own experience as a mother of seven, can test a person's reserves of tolerance. They are no more or less likely to use a gun as a tool of psychological intimidation than any other human being (and Lott suggests that "brandishing" a gun is often sufficient to quell potential violence).

More Guns Are Not the Solution

Scores of serious observers have started to suggest that teachers carry handguns to protect the school community and prevent violence. . . .

Sane and reasonable persons must find a cogent plan to increase safety and exclude violence. I do not claim to have that plan, but I do have suggestions. Teachers with guns is not one of them. . . .

Every serious assault in the schools has been planned. Days, weeks and maybe even months have been used to build a strategy of attack. The violent perpetrators would be aware of the teachers carrying firearms in the school. Those persons would be taken out first. Their weapons would be added to the arsenal of violence. You cannot protect against a cowardly, unexpected sneak attack. One gun becomes two, or three or more.

William Lenard, "Should Teachers Carry Guns?" 1999. www.gridlockmag. com.

I once taught under the leadership of a principal I thought was simply a drill sergeant, but who years later turned out to have been a child molester (although the children were older than 14).

And this was a man so strait-laced you'd have as likely expected this behavior from—well, from a priest or something.

A friend of mine who's a high school teacher also wonders what might happen if one of those not-quite-children-not-quite-adults got their hands on a teacher's weapon?

Joking, she hints that she might misplace her firearm as often as she misplaces her cell phone. Not joking, she has horrors when she thinks of the implications of a gun being stolen and used by a student with a grudge.

Schools Should Be Places to Feel Safe

But what shivers me most about teachers with guns is an even more subtle truth, one that advocates of safe schools through armed faculty might not believe.

I don't know how threatened university students in Utah feel, but there are plenty of children whose home lives are so lousy and stressful that school actually is one of the places on Earth where they feel safe.

And teachers the only adults they can trust.

Would guns change that relationship, one that often depends on vulnerability?

Would you like to take the chance, at your school?

"Too little effort has been focused on implementing balanced, rational security measures geared to the safety of the immediate environment."

Stronger Security Measures Will Make Schools Safer

Kenneth S. Trump

In the following viewpoint Kenneth S. Trump argues that while measures such as violence-prevention curriculum and conflict resolution are important methods of preventing school violence, school security is one of the most effective ways to reduce shootings in schools. In Trump's opinion, every school administrator should assess and enhance school security in order to reduce the chance of a future violent crisis occurring at his or her school. Trump is president of National School Safety and Security Services, a national firm that specializes in school security and crisis preparedness training.

As you read, consider the following questions:
1. What have steps to prevent school violence historically been focused on, according to Trump?
2. How does the author respond to the contention that safety programs in schools may be costly?
3. In Trump's opinion, why is it a good idea to conduct a security assessment before a crisis occurs?

Kenneth S. Trump, "Scared or Prepared? Reducing Risks with School Security Assessments," *The High School Magazine*, vol. 6, May/June 1999. Copyright © 1999 by *The High School Magazine*. Reproduced by permission of The National Association of Secondary Principals, www.principals.org.

Recent shifts in school violence are driving administrators in even the safest of schools and communities to realize that "it could happen here." And staff members, students, parents, politicians, lawyers, and the media want to know what you, as a school administrator, have done to prevent these things from happening.

The sad reality is that nobody can offer a 100 percent guarantee that a violent or serious security-related incident will not occur in their school. But you can and should be prepared to identify specific steps you have taken to reduce the risks of such an incident and to prepare for managing a crisis should one occur. One of the first and most often overlooked steps in this process is assessing the security of your school.

Why Assess Security?

Imagine yourself in a room in front of several hundred parents, a dozen reporters with television cameras and lights in your face, and a person asking you, "What have you done to improve security in my child's school?" Could you answer that question with confidence and sincerity? Could you list specific measures you have taken or would you stumble, mumble, and pray for the crowd to disappear?

Although even the most veteran administrator would understandably prefer to have the crowd simply disappear, more progressive administrators are now recognizing the need to take risk-reduction measures. Most steps taken to prevent school violence have historically focused on prevention-oriented measures like violence-prevention curriculum, or intervention-oriented approaches like conflict resolution. While these strategies are very important steps in a comprehensive safety plan, too little effort has been focused on implementing balanced, rational security measures geared to the safety of the immediate environment.

Too often, administrators fail to recognize that their 9:00 violence prevention curriculum and their 10:00 peer mediation program are likely to have minimal success if an 8:00 shooting occurs which could have been prevented by having better security measures in place. The three major reasons for conducting school security assessments include to:

1. Prevent and, if necessary, to prepare for effectively managing violence
2. Reduce risks and liability
3. Improve public relations by communicating your commitment to school safety prior to a crisis.

Cost of school safety programs is often a concern, but it is important to realize that good security does not always require additional manpower and equipment. School security is much more encompassing than these components alone. . . .

Inconvenience: A Small Price to Pay

Perhaps schools need to begin locking their doors. Yes, it would be an inconvenience for students, parents, teachers and others who use the school, but at least it would create an added sense of security. . . .

A lock-down alone will not prevent another tragedy, however. Schools should also study the possibility of installing metal detectors at the main entrance. Of course it would take students much longer to enter the school if they had to pass through a metal detector, but that's a small price to pay to protect our children.

Portsmouth Herald, "Time to Consider Installation of Metal Detectors at Schools," April 27, 1999.

Schools are often the safest places in the entire community—but safer than what? If 20 kids are killed in the community and 5 kids are killed in your school, is that an acceptable level of violence? Most members of your school community will clearly say no. Surveys increasingly identify security as a major concern of students, parents, and staff. And the buck stops at the school administrator's door in terms of leading the fight to create a secure environment.

Security assessments provide educational leaders with an audit of existing security conditions and recommendations for improving them at the building and district levels. Assessments also represent a balanced way of looking at school security, without the denial often present before a serious incident or the overreaction which typically follows a crisis. They also offer administrators a guide for both short and long-term security enhancements as a part of their strategic planning process for improving the school climate.

"Well meaning efforts to reduce school shootings may actually have had the unintended effect of . . . encouraging angry students to take up guns against their classmates."

Stronger Security Measures Will Make Schools Less Safe

James Alan Fox and Jack Levin

In the following viewpoint James Alan Fox and Jack Levin argue that too much focus on improving school security may actually inspire future violence rather than prevent it. In their opinion, when schools react to shootings by increasing security they inadvertently remind students that school shootings are one avenue for expressing their anger and alienation. Fox is the Lipman Family Professor of Criminal Justice and Levin is the Brudnick Professor of Sociology and Criminology at Northwestern University in Illinois.

As you read, consider the following questions:
1. While most children identify with the pain of school-shooting victims, what do some alienated youngsters see, as argued by the authors?
2. What is the core problem at many schools, according to Fox and Levin?
3. In the authors' opinion, what is the silver lining in America's concerns over terrorism and the war in Iraq?

James Alan Fox and Jack Levin, "Perpetuating School Violence," *District Administration*, vol. 40, May 2004, p. 79. Copyright © 2004 by the Professional Media Group. Reproduced by permission.

Although images of the 1999 Columbine massacre[1] are still fresh in our minds, we appear to have turned the corner in the struggle to control school violence.

Five years ago [1999], it seemed as though there was no end in sight to the growing threat of schoolyard terror. Survey after survey indicated that school safety was the most critical issue for parents, well ahead of concerns over curriculum quality or the availability of educational resources.

Amidst a pervasive state of alarm, many administrators responded by turning their schools into armed camps. They upgraded security and sought to identify potentially violent students by scanning for warning signs such as black trenchcoats or bullying. More and more students passed through metal detectors and were repeatedly reminded to be on the lookout for anyone uttering a threat.

Oddly, well meaning efforts to reduce school shootings may actually have had the unintended effect of intensifying fear in vulnerable students while encouraging angry students to take up guns against their classmates. These practices inadvertently reminded vengeful students around the country about one particular way to resolve their problems. Violence against classmates had become, if not an accepted way, at least a familiar way to respond to classroom bullies. The attention we paid to school violence only reinforced that notion.

The Evolution of School Violence

While most children identify with the pain of the victims, a few alienated youngsters identify more with the power of the perpetrators. They see school shooters not as villains but as heroes. Not only did they get even with the nasty bullies and insensitive teachers, but they're famous for it.

In many respects, the problems students face today are no different than earlier generations. There have been schoolyard bullies as long as there have been schools; there has been adolescent alienation as long as there have been teenagers.

Yet, earlier generations of disgruntled youngsters responded in less violent ways. School homicides committed

---

1. Two students went on a shooting rampage at Columbine High School in Littleton, Colorado, killing twelve other students and a teacher, and injuring twenty-three.

School Shootings Around the World

March 13, 1996 Dunblane, Scotland	16 children and one teacher killed at Dunblane Primary School by Thomas Hamilton, who then killed himself. 10 others wounded in attack.
Feb. 19, 1997 Bethel, Alaska	Principal and one student killed, two others wounded by Evan Ramsey, 16.
March 1997 Sanaa, Yemen	Eight people (six students and two others) at two schools killed by Mohammad Ah-man al-Naziri.
April 28, 1999 Taber, Alberta, Canada	One student killed, one wounded at W.R. Myers High School in first fatal high school shooting in Canada in 20 years. The suspect, a 14-year-old-boy, had dropped out of school after he was severely ostracized by his classmates.
Dec. 7, 1999 Veghel, Netherlands	One teacher and three students wounded by a 17-year-old student.
Jan. 18, 2001 Jan, Sweden	One student killed by two boys, ages 17 and 19.
Feb. 19, 2002 Freising, Germany	Two killed in Eching by a man at the factory from which he had been fired; he then traveled to Freising and killed the headmaster of the technical school from which he had been expelled. He also wounded another teacher before killing himself.
April 26, 2002 Erfurt, Germany	13 teachers, two students, and one police-man killed, ten wounded by Robert Stein-haeuser, 19, at the Johann Gutenburg sec-ondary school. Steinhaeuser then killed himself.
April 29, 2002 Viasenica, Bosnia- Herzegovina	One teacher killed, one wounded by Dragoslav Petkovic, 17, who then killed himself.

"A Time Line of Recent Worldwide School Shootings," 2004. www.info please.com.

by teenagers a decade ago were isolated cases of mostly one-on-one attacks. They didn't make the national news.

We are not suggesting that the problem of school violence be ignored. Rather, educators must learn to respond to a violent episode without gratuitously calling so much direct attention to it. We should focus on the causes of school violence

—a disrespectful climate, large and impersonal schools and bullying—without continually reinforcing the symptoms.

The core problem at many schools is a lack of any sense of community. Too many students are nameless faces to teachers, psychologists and guidance counselors, whose huge caseloads in oversized schools do not permit them to know their students as individuals. If we really want to assess students for violent tendencies, we have to get to know them better. We should deal with the troubled student long before he or she becomes troublesome.

Examining the Cause and Effect

Why then the sudden drop in episodes of school shootings since Columbine? Could it be that our security efforts and zero-tolerance policies have been so successful? Or, could it be instead that the contagion effect has run its course?

It is perhaps a silver lining to America's concern in recent years over international terrorism—from [terrorist group] Al Qaeda to anthrax—as well as about the war in Iraq. Such concerns have shifted attention away from school violence, thus allowing teachers to teach and students to learn without constantly fixating on school shootings and reinforcing the contagion.

At the same time, today's calm is a fragile one. Should some angry 14-year-old in Smalltown High decide to "do a Columbine," the hysteria would quickly resurface as would the threat of copycat behavior—that is, of course, unless we respond with good sense and reason.

"Experts have long believed that helping kids adjust and get settled into a community is important in reducing recidivism."

Helping Juvenile Offenders Reenter Their Communities After Incarceration Can Reduce Crime

Steve Christian

In the following viewpoint Steve Christian maintains that many incarcerated youth have trouble making the transition from prison to their home environments and often return to crime. Providing these youth with support—such as help with job searches, parenting, housing, and drug addictions—before and after they are released increases the likelihood that they will stay out of jail, explains Christian. Christian covers child welfare and youth issues for the National Conference of State Legislatures, an organization that provides policy makers with research and technical assistance.

As you read, consider the following questions:

1. How many juvenile offenders are released every year, according to Christian?
2. According to the Florida Department of Juvenile Justice, what was the amount saved by a 4 percent reduction in recidivism between 1997 and 1999?
3. What did the TRACS study show about young offenders who became "engaged" in work or school immediately after release?

Steve Christian, "Out of Lock-Up: Now What?" *State Legislatures*, vol. 29, December 2003, p. 21. Copyright © 2003 by the National Conference of State Legislatures. Reproduced by permission.

Johnny is a soft-spoken 19-year-old who is finishing a year at Lookout Mountain Youth Services Center in Golden, Colo., a high-security juvenile correctional facility that houses some of the state's toughest kids. He has a long arrest record for stealing and selling drugs. Before he came to Lookout Mountain, he escaped from a state institution in Pueblo, stole a car and was on the run for two years. In addition to his criminal record, he had a cocaine addiction and no high school diploma.

Johnny will be going home shortly, but his family will not be there to welcome him. His father is hiding from the law after violating parole; his younger sister ran away from a group home; his older sister was recently arrested for selling drugs; his older brother is in prison; and he doesn't know where his mother is.

Despite all of this, Johnny has hope for the future. In the past year at Lookout, he earned his GED [the equivalent of a high school diploma], kicked his drug habit and took vocational training. He plans to live with his girlfriend, with whom he fathered a child. He says her parents give him the support and guidance he never got from his own family.

But staying out of trouble will not be easy. His biggest challenge? "Drugs," he says without hesitation. "When I visit friends, I see them doing drugs. I see their parents doing drugs." Finding a decent job, he says, will be the best protection against relapse. That and regular contact with his probation officer.

The most important thing he got out of his stay at Lookout Mountain, he says, is the motivation to succeed. The big question for Johnny and for thousands of other young people leaving confinement is whether that newfound motivation can survive in rough neighborhoods where drugs, crime and unemployment are pervasive.

Reducing Recidivism

About 100,000 juvenile offenders are released every year, according to the Department of Justice. A large percentage of them had serious drug and mental health problems when they were incarcerated.

Kids in confinement are much more likely to have had serious problems with hard drugs, hallucinogens and designer drugs than are kids who get into trouble, but avoid incarceration, says Troy Armstrong at the Center for Delinquency and Crime Policy Studies, California State University. After release, many of them commit new crimes and end up back in jail. A Department of Justice study of prisoners released in 1994 found that more than 82 percent of those under age 18 were rearrested within three years, and more than 55 percent were reconvicted.

Recidivism—returning to jail—is, of course, expensive. It costs about $135 per day to keep a youthful offender incarcerated, according to the Department of Justice. But that is only part of the story. Armstrong says many released youths are chronic offenders who will go on to commit serious crimes that carry heavy costs. Reaching just a few of them can yield significant savings. The Florida Department of Juvenile Justice found that a 4 percent reduction in recidivism between FY [Fiscal Year] 1997 and 1999 resulted in almost $65 million in avoided costs to victims and criminal justice agencies.

Although practice varies from state to state, many juvenile justice systems focus much of their post-release efforts on surveillance and monitoring (in other words, checking to ensure the offender is meeting the conditions of release), rather than on supporting kids during the difficult process of returning to society. In many places, young people leave jail unprepared to make the transition from a highly structured institutional environment to an unstructured and often chaotic home environment. And there's not enough help for them in the community to reinforce any gains they made while in confinement.

Part of the problem is a lack of coordination among the juvenile justice, school, mental health, drug treatment and court systems.

Experts have long believed that helping kids adjust and get settled into a community is important in reducing recidivism. The Intensive Aftercare Program (IAP) developed over the past 15 years by Armstrong and David Altschuler of Johns Hopkins University is a widely recognized model that was tested at sites in three states over a five-year period. Key to the program are the intensive services juveniles get before release and once they return to the community. Kids get help with drug and alcohol addictions, mental health problems, job searches, parenting, housing and living on their own.

Costs vary. An analysis by the Washington State Institute for Public Policy estimated in 2002 that the state's intensive parole program, based on the IAP model, cost $28.09 per day for an average of nine months ($7,785), compared with $12.22 per day for regular parole for lower risk youth.

Unfortunately, there are only a handful of studies on juvenile re-entry programs, and they have shown little or no effect on recidivism rates. The existing research, however, is largely inconclusive on whether these programs are worth the cost. Some of the studies suggest that the discouraging results could be due to poor implementation of otherwise theoretically sound models. The most comprehensive study of juvenile re-entry, the evaluation of IAP in Colorado, Nevada and Virginia will be released in early 2004. That study, says Armstrong, is inconclusive because of small sample sizes and gaps in data collection. Another evaluation that is just getting started will likely yield more useful information. That study will be examining outcomes of a program run by the Boys and Girls Clubs of America called the Targeted Re-Entry Project, an 11-site pilot project based on the IAP model.

David Bennett, central region director for the Colorado Division of Youth Corrections, believes the IAP experiment in Colorado was well worth the effort, even if he can't document a significant reduction in recidivism.

"It accomplished a major culture change within Lookout Mountain," he says. "When kids are in an institution, it's easy to keep everything under the control of the institution. IAP made us do a better job of working with organizations in the community" to prepare kids for release. "It's also made the campus much more family friendly." Bennett believes the most important part of re-entry planning is supporting families and helping them take the lead role in a juvenile's return to the community.

Another unexpected benefit of the Colorado pilot program was a reduction in lengths of stay. "The experimental group left the institution an average of three months sooner than the control group," says Bennett. "That has resulted in cost savings for the state."

A New Focus on School

Education for young ex-offenders is getting more attention at both the state and federal levels. Although national data are hard to come by, anecdotal evidence suggests that youths leaving detention do poorly in school and often drop out.

In 1997, the California Legislature created grants for county offices of education to support comprehensive, multi-agency plans for first-time juvenile offenders on probation and those coming from county-run juvenile camps, ranches and halls.

The program, known as the High-Risk Youth Education and Public Safety Program, has been "very successful," according to Bill Lane, education programs consultant for the state Department of Education. The final evaluation of the program by Armstrong and his colleagues at California State University will not be completed until early next year [2004]. Preliminary results, however, "are looking promising," says Armstrong. "They show a marked reduction in the level of risk factors" that affect school attendance, dropout rates and academic performance, he says. He also notes that the early findings suggest a reduction in recidivism among young people participating in the project.

At the suggestion of a legislatively mandated task force, Maine passed a measure in 2001 to improve the success of juvenile offenders returning to local schools. Phil McCarthy, a legislative analyst who staffed the task force, says one of the major barriers was reluctance of schools to accept ex-offenders without having sufficient information about their substance abuse and mental health histories. The legislation requires the development of statewide standards for enrolling juvenile offenders in local school systems. It also calls for the creation of teams to help the process.

Education for youthful offenders is a major emphasis of Title 1, Part D, of the No Child Left Behind Act, which provides about $48 million for children who are neglected, delinquent or at-risk. States must use between 15 percent and 30 percent of their grants to help young offenders get back in school successfully or get college or vocational training if they have graduated.

The Importance of Engagement

Researchers at the University of Oregon recently studied more than 500 young people who were released from the custody of the Oregon Youth Authority. More than half had a special education disability, and about 40 percent also had a psychiatric disability. The study, known as the TRACS Project, confirmed high recidivism and low employment and school enrollment rates, particularly for the kids with disabilities.

The study also contained some good news. If a young offender remained in the community for one year following release, it was virtually certain that he would not return to the correctional system. Moreover, young offenders who had become "engaged" in work or school immediately after release tended to stay out of trouble at much higher rates than those who did not. These positive effects were especially pronounced for kids with disabilities.

From the TRACS study evolved Oregon's Project SUPPORT, which provides individualized services to incarcerated youths with disabilities. A transition specialist helps each kid get into school or find a job quickly after release. Although the program has not been rigorously evaluated, a look at statistics is encouraging. Data from April 2003 show that 68.2 percent of Project SUPPORT participants were in school or had a job at six months after getting out, with only 16.6 percent back in custody, compared with 46.7 percent and 29.3 percent, respectively, of youths in the TRACS study.

"We are encouraged by the early data on Project SUPPORT and are looking forward to a more complete evaluation," says Oregon Representative Max Williams. "It's really common sense that with no job or no assistance in getting back to school, a lot of these kids will fall back into the same behaviors that got them into custody in the first place. While transition services are expensive, in the long run we hope they will improve the future for these young people, reduce victimization and save money on future costs of custody.". . .

The Challenge of Re-Entry

Sending juveniles back to the community is a challenge, both for the kids who leave institutions and for the public systems that are responsible for reducing juvenile crime. For young offenders, going home means facing the temptation of drugs and crime. For the juvenile justice system, it means coordinating the efforts of agencies and systems that don't often work together. Bennett, for one, thinks the effort is worth it. "In spite of our best efforts, we think it's pretty certain that this population is a public safety risk," he says. "Many of them have missed out on the normal process of socialization. Even people with good family resources aren't fully independent until their mid-20s. Our kids have weak parental support. We've got to prop them up."

> *"Our goal cannot simply be returning youthful offenders to society, but it must also include helping to ensure that there are not others to take their place within our facilities."*

Helping Juvenile Offenders Avoid Incarceration Can Reduce Crime

James A. Gondles Jr.

In the following viewpoint James A. Gondles Jr. asserts that while helping juvenile offenders reenter communities upon release from detention facilities is important, the best way to reduce juvenile crime is to prevent juveniles from being jailed in the first place. A major part of this approach is preventing drug and alcohol abuse, argues Gondles, since involvement with these substances often leads to juvenile crime. Gondles is executive director of the American Correctional Association, the largest international correctional association in the world.

As you read, consider the following questions:
1. In what way do juveniles live in a different world than did previous generations, in Gondles's opinion?
2. In 1998 how many high school seniors reported trying alcohol and illicit drugs, according to the author?
3. According to Gondles, what are some of the ways society can prevent juvenile crime?

Growing up in Ponca City, Okla., I did not confront many of the issues that today's youths face. I was not exposed to drugs such as GHB (gamma hydroxybutyrate) and methamphetamines as today's youths are. I was not exposed to the influence of gangs. And I did not see celebrities from the world of sports being accused of violent crimes or of using drugs, including steroids. It is safe to say that the world has changed.

Juveniles Face Complex Problems

Juveniles in the United States today live in a world much different from that of my generation. Problems experienced by children now are the products of multiple and sometimes complex sources. Fewer children are raised in two-parent homes. And although the proportion of juveniles living in poverty has recently declined, they still are far more likely to live in poverty today than 20 years ago. Drug and alcohol use is more common and gang involvement has increased.

In 1998, the most recent year statistics are available, more than 81 percent of high school seniors reported trying alcohol and more than half reported using alcohol within the past 30 days. Also in 1998, 54 percent of all seniors said they had at least tried illicit drugs, with marijuana being the most commonly used illicit drug by far.

While self-reported drug and alcohol use among juveniles has remained stable or only increased slightly during the 1990s, the juvenile arrest rate for drug abuse violations nearly doubled between 1992 and 1996. This reflects a greater effort by law enforcement, as well as by the community, to crack down on illegal drug and alcohol use by our nation's youths.

Large Number of Juvenile Offenders

As with the adult population, a large percentage of juveniles who come into contact with the criminal justice system do so because of their involvement with drugs and alcohol. The proportion of high school seniors who reported breaking the law (for something other than using alcohol or drugs) was greater among drug users than nonusers.

More juveniles come into contact with the nation's criminal justice system today than at any time in our nation's his-

A Downward Spiral

Many youthful offenders begin their involvement in criminal behaviors at an early age. Parents and the community begin to lose them as their success in school begins to decline. School serves as a stabilizer for many youthful offenders who are already disadvantaged as a result of broken families and/or poor or nonexistent home environments. When schools become nonresponsive to their needs, their delinquent behavior escalates. As they move through adolescence, they become more and more detached from the systems and culture that would normally help them maintain their stability in the community. . . .

These are challenging times for adolescents. Communities, either out of fear or lack of knowledge, ignore these youths' numerous cries for help and generally regard them as bad or incorrigible. Their parents or other significant family members begin to feel as if they are in a maze with no way out. The adolescents' negative behavior continues to escalate and the system continues to be insensitive and punitive. Experience has shown that much of this negative, self-destructive, and/or violent behavior is a facade to hide problems youths are facing.

Once these youthful offenders interface with the adult correctional system, the challenge of managing them shifts from the community to the penal system. The Department of Corrections has the awesome responsibility of developing programs to habilitate and return them to society as productive law-abiding citizens.

Kathy Bryant-Thompson, Deloris Glymph, and William Sturgeon, *Corrections Today*, October 2002.

---

tory. According to the U.S. Department of Justice Office of Juvenile Justice and Delinquency Prevention, law enforcement agencies in the United States made 2.8 million arrests of individuals younger than 18 in 1997. Between 1987 and 1994, the female juvenile violent crime arrest rate more than doubled, while the male rate increased by two-thirds. These arrests led to more than 5,600 individuals younger than 18—nearly 2 percent of all new court commitments—being sent to the nation's adult prison systems.

Daunting Challenges

Given the additional issues that youthful offenders present, the challenges to our profession [criminal justice] are daunting. We can ensure that youthful offenders have access to resources that will help prevent them from returning to lives of crime following their release from correctional institutions. We must make a greater effort to improve the quality of our rehabilitation, job training and re-entry initiatives. The challenges associated with this are great. And meeting them is only part of our obligation as criminal justice professionals.

The Importance of Prevention

As a society, we cannot legislate morality. We cannot force our nation's youths to live alcohol-, drug- and crime-free lives. As such, there will always be juvenile crime, and some of it will require youths to be incarcerated. However, our responsibility for youthful offenders cannot begin once a juvenile enters the criminal justice system. It must begin in the community, even before a youth comes into contact with the criminal justice system. Society must work to improve the quality of and access to after-school programs, taking children off the streets during the times of day when the majority of crimes committed by youthful offenders occur. We can ensure that these programs provide information about the dangers of alcohol and drug use; after all, studies show that information on the dangers of drugs and alcohol have a significant impact on use among youths. Our goal cannot simply be returning youthful offenders to society, but it must also include helping to ensure that there are not others to take their place within our facilities. It's a daunting challenge, one that most would not believe is our responsibility. But I believe that we have a role to play, and I refuse to believe that the goal of eliminating juvenile crime is out of our reach.

Periodical Bibliography

The following articles have been selected to supplement the diverse views presented in this chapter.

Larry Bellinger   "Scared Crooked," *Sojourners*, September 2001.

Judith A. Browne   "Racial Profiling in School?" *Essence*, January 2001.

Kathy Bryant-   "Youthful Offenders: Today's Challenges,
Thomson, Deloris   Tomorrow's Leaders?" *Corrections Today*,
Glymph, and   October 2002.
William Sturgeon

Robert J. Caldwell   "Gun Laws Cannot Stop a Killer's Rampage,"
                           San Diego Union-Tribune, March 11, 2001.

Lili Frank Garfinkel   "Promoting Better Interaction Between
and Renelle Nelson   Juvenile Court, Schools, and Parents,"
                           Reclaiming Children and Youth, Spring 2004.

Globe & Mail   "The Right Penalties for Teenage Offenders,"
                           May 5, 2003.

*Harvard Mental   "Scared Crooked," January 2003.
Health Letter*

Eric Lichtblau   "FBI Urges Educators to Spot Signs of
                           Violence," *Los Angeles Times*, September 7,
                           2000.

Kandice Morgan   "Scared Straight," *Essence*, December 2002.
and Glenda Hatchett

Helene Mulholland   "Restorative Justice: Pulling No Punches with
                           School Bullies," *Guardian*, June 9, 2004.

Wayne W. Munson   "Recreation and Juvenile Delinquency
                           Prevention: How Recreation Professionals Can
                           Design Programs That Really Work," *Parks
                           and Recreation*, June 1, 2002.

Anthony J. Petrosino   "How Can We Respond Effectively to Juvenile
                           Crime?" *Pediatrics*, March 1, 2000.

Pete du Pont   "Restorative Justice an Alternative to Jail,"
                           Human Events, March 19, 2001.

Carter White   "Reclaiming Incarcerated Youth Through
                           Education," *Corrections Today*, April 2002.

CHAPTER 4

How Can the U.S. Juvenile Justice System Be Improved?

Chapter Preface

Over the last two hundred years, attitudes toward juvenile justice in the United States have fluctuated between the belief that young criminals should be treated harshly and the idea that society should strive to rehabilitate juveniles. In the 1800s juvenile criminals in the United States received the same punishment as adult criminals—they were tried in the same courts and housed in the same jails. At the beginning of the twentieth century, however, the first U.S. juvenile courts were created to end this long-standing practice. These new courts were based on the belief that because children are still developing they should not bear the same responsibility as adults for their actions. As author Fox Butterfield explains, "Children were thought to be still susceptible to rehabilitation, and the judges were to act informally. Serving like doctors, to dispense the right treatment for offenders rather than punishment."

At the end of the twentieth century, the American attitude toward juvenile crime changed again. As criminal acts by youth were seen as increasingly common and serious, many Americans began to believe that punishing children as adults might be the most effective way to prevent juvenile crime. According to author Edward Humes, "With juveniles increasingly responsible for major and violent crimes, public sentiment in support of a separate justice system for children has been waning, replaced by frustration at the system's inability to quickly and resolutely deal with out-of-control delinquents."

Both approaches to juvenile crime have staunch advocates. Those in favor of rehabilitation, such as writer Lane Nelson, argue that in the majority of cases, delinquent youth can be made into law-abiding citizens. According to Nelson, "As study after study has shown, only a few kids are lost forever. Most troubled youth can be salvaged." These advocates argue that jailing juvenile criminals may actually cause them to commit future crimes. Other analysts, such as Los Angeles County District Attorney Gil Garcetti, contend that "juvenile crime has been rising unacceptably fast, and kids learn they can get away with it because there is no real punishment for the first few crimes." People such as Garcetti believe that the threat of harsh punishment is the only way to deter juvenile crime.

In addition to the debate over rehabilitation versus punishment, there is debate over many other elements of the U.S. juvenile justice system. One thing these commentators have in common, though, is the belief that the system can be made better. The authors in the following chapter present various views on how the U.S. juvenile justice system can be improved.

> "While 'Equal Justice Under Law' is the
> foundation of our legal system . . . the
> juvenile justice system is anything but
> equal."

The Juvenile Justice System Must Stop Discriminating Against Minority Youth

Eileen Poe-Yamagata and Michael A. Jones

In the following viewpoint Eileen Poe-Yamagata and Michael A. Jones argue that minority youth—especially African Americans—receive unequal treatment at every stage of the juvenile justice process. According to Poe-Yamagata and Jones, minorities are arrested and confined in juvenile correctional facilities at rates disproportionate to their representation in the general population. Moreover, even when they commit the same crimes as white youth, minority youth are sent to adult courts with greater frequency, the authors contend. They advocate a nationwide effort to identify the causes of this trend and to take steps to change it. Poe-Yamagata and Jones are senior researchers with the National Council on Crime and Delinquency.

As you read, consider the following questions:

1. At what stage of the juvenile justice system is racial disparity most pronounced, according to the authors?
2. According to Poe-Yamagata and Jones, how much more likely were African American youth to be detained for a drug offense than other youth?

There has been growing national concern about the over-representation of minority youth (traditionally defined as African American, Native American, Latino, and Asians) confined in secure facilities. Research has shown that minority youth, and in particular African Americans, are confined in public correctional facilities at rates disproportionate to their representation in the general population. Disproportionate minority confinement (DMC), as defined by the Juvenile Justice and Delinquency Prevention Act refers to a situation in which the minority proportion of juveniles detained or confined in secure detention facilities, secure correctional facilities, jails, and lockups exceeds the proportion of such groups in the general population. While public attention may have focused on the disproportionate number of minorities in confinement, minority overrepresentation is often a product of actions that occur at earlier points in the juvenile justice system.

Critical Decision Points

In order to put the representation of minority youth in context it is necessary to view the justice system as a process. Representation of minority youth can be examined as a series of critical decision points as youth progress through the system. Accordingly, amendments to the Juvenile Justice and Delinquency Prevention Act required states to assess the level of minority youth confinement in their juvenile justice systems by systematically identifying the extent of overrepresentation at each decision point in the process. This systematic approach views the overall process that creates overrepresentation rather than focusing only on the end result of confinement.

Depending on local practices and traditions, states and communities can differ in the way that they process juvenile law violators. However, a common set of critical decision points regarding arrest, intake, detention, adjudication, and disposition have become the cornerstone for researchers' examination of minority overrepresentation.

Studies finding evidence of disproportionate minority confinement typically ascribe its causes to either racial bias against minority youth within the juvenile justice system or more serious and/or more frequent offenses being committed by minority youth. Determining whether either or both of these phenomenon are the reason for disparity requires analysis of detailed data providing information on specific offense classifications, criminal history, and other factors used in decision-making. Studies such as this suggest that processing decisions in many states and local juvenile justice systems are not racially neutral. Minority youth are more likely than White youth to become involved in the system with their overrepresentation increasing at each stage of the process.

Wilkinson. © 2000 by Signe Wilkinson and Cartoonist & Writers Syndicate. Reproduced by permission.

Research also suggests that disparity is most pronounced at the beginning stages of involvement with the juvenile justice system or, more specifically, at the intake and detention decision points. When racial/ethnic differences are found, they tend to accumulate as youth are processed through the system. This "cumulative disadvantage" of minority youth within the juvenile justice system is reflected in a 1997 report on DMC which found that overrepresentation increased from the point of arrest through other points in the system to the final point of secure (juvenile) corrections in 31 of 36 states studied. The first [juvenile justice advocate] *Building Blocks for Youth* report, "The Color of Justice," found a similar "cumulative disadvantage" for youth in California who were waived to adult court and sentenced to prison.

As expected, much of the existing research on DMC has

primarily focused on disparity in the processing of youth through the juvenile court and the disproportionate confinement of minority youth in facilities while under juvenile court jurisdiction. However, with lawmakers across the country actively pursuing measures to "get tough" on serious and violent juvenile offending, increasing numbers of juveniles are being processed through adult criminal courts. Currently [2002], all states and the District of Columbia allow adult criminal prosecution of juveniles under some circumstance. In addition, between 1992 and 1997, legislatures in 47 states and the District of Columbia enacted laws that either made it easier to transfer youth from the juvenile justice system to the criminal justice system, that gave criminal and juvenile courts expanded sentencing options, or modified or removed traditional juvenile court confidentiality provisions.

As a result, the consequences of disproportionate numbers of minority youth flowing through the juvenile justice system is no longer just about juvenile court sanctions. It is now also about disproportionate numbers of minority youth subject to adult court processing and incarceration in adult jails and prisons. A 1998 report showed that African American youth were less than one-half (41%) of cases involving a juvenile charged with a felony and processed through the juvenile justice system but two-thirds (67%) of such cases transferred from juvenile court jurisdiction and handled in the criminal justice system. Almost two-thirds of all juveniles transferred on a felony charge were convicted in adult court and about two-thirds of these convictions involved incarceration—49% in adult prison and 19% in adult jails. Indeed, a recent study by the Bureau of Justice Statistics of the U.S. Department of Justice reports that the number of people under age 18 who are sentenced to adult state prisons each year more than doubled between 1985 and 1997—from 3,400 to 7,400. . . .

The Arrest

Police are typically the first officials of the justice system that a youth encounters. Responses range from a simple warning, to arrest and detention, to transfer to adult court.

Decisions by law enforcement are pivotal in determining the profile of cases formally involved in the juvenile justice system. At arrest, a decision is made to either send the matter further into the justice system or to divert the matter, usually into alternative programs. In 1997, about two-thirds of all juvenile arrests were referred to juvenile court, one-quarter were handled within the department and released, less than one in 10 were referred to adult court, and the remainder were referred to another agency.

United States law enforcement agencies made an estimated 2.6 million arrests of persons under age 18 in 1998. Less than 5% of those arrests were for Violent Crime Index offenses, and less than one tenth of 1% were for murder.

The majority (71%) of those arrests involved White youth. Still, African American youth were overrepresented in most offense categories. . . .

Juvenile Court Processing

Most delinquency cases are referred to juvenile court by law enforcement while others are made by parents, victims, schools, and probation officers. At court intake a decision— typically made by either juvenile probation or a prosecutor's office—is made to either dismiss the case, handle the matter informally, or request formal intervention by the juvenile court. . . .

In 1997, the majority of cases referred to juvenile court involved White youth. The proportion of referred cases involving African American youth was twice their proportion in the population. Of the estimated 1,755,100 delinquency cases referred to the nation's juvenile courts in 1997, 66% involved White youth, 31% involved African American youth, and 3% involved youth of other races. . . .

An estimated 326,800 delinquent youth were detained in 1997. With respect to their proportion in the referral population, White youth were underrepresented while African American youth were overrepresented in the detained population. Of White youth referred to juvenile court, a smaller percentage were locked up in detention facilities (66% referred vs. 53% detained). Of African American youth referred to juvenile court, a larger percentage were locked up in detention facilities (31% vs. 44%). Youth of other races had the same percentage of referred and detained cases (3%).

This pattern of disproportion was across all offense categories but was most dramatic among drug offense cases. Cases involving White youth were 66% of those referred but only 44% of those detained. In contrast, drug offense cases involving African American youth were 32% of those referred but 55% of those detained. In every offense category, a substantially greater percentage of African American youth were detained than White youth.

Overall, detention was used more often for African American youth (27%) and youth of other races (19%) than for White youth (15%). This was true among each of the four major offense categories as well. Thus, for youth charged with comparable offenses—whether person, property, drug, or public order offenses—minority youth, especially African American youth, were locked up in detention more often than White youth.

Consequently, cases involving African American youth were more than twice as likely to be detained for a drug offense than were cases involving White youth or youth of other races (38%, 14%, and 16%, respectively). . . .

Waiver

An estimated 8,400 petitioned delinquency cases were judicially waived from juvenile to adult court in 1997. This represents about 1% of all petitioned cases. Overall, cases involving White youth represented a smaller proportion of waived cases than of petitioned cases (50% vs. 63%). In contrast, cases involving African American youth represented a larger proportion of waived cases than petitioned cases (46% vs. 34%). . . .

Minority youth were much more likely than White youth to be waived to criminal court even when charged with a similar offense. This was true for every offense category. Again, the differences are particularly striking for person and drug offenses. In 1997, 1.2% of the White youth charged with person offenses were waived to adult court, while 1.8% of the African American youth were waived, and 2.4% of other minorities were waived. Similarly, .7% of White youth charged with drug offenses was waived to adult court, while 1.8% of African American and 1.3% of other minority youth were waived. . . .

Public Versus Private Facilities

Public juvenile facilities are typically locked local detention facilities or locked state correctional institutions. Private juvenile facilities are often less restrictive and less prison-like. Minorities represented a greater proportion of youth in public (66%) than private (54%) facilities, and the minority proportion of youth in public facilities was almost twice the White proportion (66% vs. 34%). Among Latinos, the proportion of detained and committed youth in public facilities was almost double the proportion in private facilities (21% vs. 11%). . . .

"Separate but Unequal"

Historically, the most punitive and restrictive sanction facing youth charged with a criminal offense involved court-ordered placement in a residential facility—particularly public training schools. The recent past, however, has revealed growing sentiment away from the early juvenile court's original goals of diversion and treatment towards punishment, accountability and public safety. In addition, state legislatures are increasingly moving away from case-specific decisions to transfer juveniles to criminal court in favor of transfer decisions based on the offender's age or offense seriousness.

As the blurring of the line between juvenile and criminal court increases, so does the likelihood that these trends will disproportionately affect minority youth. Already, African American juveniles are overrepresented with respect to their proportion in the population at every decision point in the process. African Americans were:

- 15% of youth under age 18.
- 26% of juvenile arrests.
- 31% of referrals to juvenile court.
- 44% of the detained population.
- 34% of youth formally processed by the juvenile court.
- 32% of youth adjudicated delinquent.
- 46% of youth judicially waived to criminal court.
- 40% of youth in residential placement.
- 58% of youth admitted to state adult prison.

Unfortunately, the cumulative disadvantage of minority youth will continue to spiral as states continue to pass more punitive laws allowing youth to be charged as adults and, therefore, subject to adult sanctions such as prison and the death penalty. Thus, as legislative trends push beyond the boundary of juvenile justice, the continued amplification of minority youth in the system—as well as the consequences resulting from such a system—will continue as well, unless significant action is taken at the federal, state and local levels.

While "Equal Justice Under Law" is the foundation of our legal system, and is carved on the front of the U.S. Supreme Court, the juvenile justice system is anything but equal. However, throughout the system, minority youth—especially African American youth—receive different and harsher treatment. This is true even when White youth and minority youth are charged with similar offenses. This report documents a juvenile justice system that is "separate but unequal."

It is time for a nationwide effort to identify the causes of this differential treatment of minority youth and a concerted campaign to provide a fair and equal justice system for our youth.

"*When black and white criminals are carefully compared . . . the justice system treats them pretty much the same.*"

Discrimination Against Minority Youth in the Juvenile Justice System Is Not a Problem

Jared Taylor

In the following viewpoint Jared Taylor argues against claims that the juvenile justice system discriminates against minorities. Claims of racial bias are not supported by evidence, maintains Taylor; instead, the evidence actually shows equal treatment of African American and white criminals. In his opinion, African American youth are overrepresented in jails simply because they commit more crimes than do white youth. Taylor is president of the New Century Foundation, a think tank in Washington, D.C., and frequently writes on crime and crime rates.

As you read, consider the following questions:

1. According to the author, what does the Building Blocks for Youth report say about incarceration of juveniles in 1993?
2. In Taylor's opinion, how did the press distort the Building Blocks for Youth report findings?
3. Why is Building Blocks for Youth unlikely to issue a correction, according to Taylor?

"**A** black youth is six times more likely to be locked up than a white peer, even when charged with a similar crime and when neither has a record. . . ." So began an April 25 [2000] *Associated Press* news story picked up uncritically by dozens of papers including *The Washington Post* that helped feed a wave of national breast-beating over the unfairness of the juvenile justice system. The story was about a report put out by a San Francisco organization called Building Blocks for Youth, which claimed to "document the cumulative disadvantage of minority youth" in the face of a biased system.

The Building Blocks for Youth Report

But is the system really that bad? Are black first-time offenders really six times more likely to go to jail than white first-timers charged with the same crimes? Of course not. To its credit, the Building Blocks for Youth report didn't actually say that. To its great discredit the organization has done nothing to dispel an error that perfectly suits its image of prejudiced law-enforcement. The "six times" figure is probably well on its way into the folklore of racial oppression.

What the report says is that during 1993, black juveniles in several states were six times more likely than whites to get locked up in some kind of public facility. It says nothing about what accounts for this six-fold disparity. This finding is vastly different from the claim that made headlines, namely, that blacks are six times more likely than whites to go to jail when they commit the same crimes and have similar records. The mere fact that more blacks than whites are locked up is something criminologists have known for years and does not necessarily suggest justice system bias at all. It may reflect only higher crime rates among blacks.

Media Mischief

The media mischief began when this bit of data was bulleted as a "major finding" at the beginning of the report: "When White youth and minority youth were charged with the same offenses, African-American youth with no prior admissions were six times more likely to be incarcerated in public facilities than White youth with the same background." It sure sounds like a stacked deck in court.

"Perhaps the wording in the bullet was misleading," concedes Eileen Poe-Yamagata, one of the report's co-authors. It sure was. It misled nearly every journalist in the country. The *Boston Herald* wrote that "black first-time offenders are six times more likely to be sentenced to prison by juvenile courts than whites." The *Saint Louis Post-Dispatch* led its story with the same shocking finding. The *Chicago Tribune, Cincinnati Enquirer, Cleveland Plain-Dealer* and *Seattle Post-Intelligencer* and plenty of other papers trumpeted the news. [Journalist] William Raspberry agonized over judicial bias in his column. The *Philadelphia Inquirer* wrung its hands over the six times problem in an editorial. It was a startling, incendiary finding and most of the press swallowed it without a gurgle. The *Washington Times* was one of only a handful of newspapers that did not join the pack, baying about racism.

No Evidence of Racial Bias

If there really were such strong evidence of racial bias in the justice system it would be newsworthy all right, but that is not what the report found because it is not there to be found. Many studies over the years have determined that when black and white criminals are carefully compared for offense and criminal record, the justice system treats them pretty much the same. As for high rates of incarceration for blacks, compelling evidence from the U.S. government's National Crime Victimization Survey suggests that blacks—juvenile and adult—are overrepresented in jails because they commit more crimes, not because of judicial bias.

What are the chances Building Blocks for Youth will issue

a correction? "We're not really sure at this point," says Miss Poe-Yamagata. "I had noticed in a few of the articles that there could be a need for that, but there hasn't been an official decision on that." Don't count on one anytime soon. Groups like this thrive on charges of racism, not on sober reporting. It is not likely to be much bothered if a disparity in lock-up rates that probably reflects nothing more than high crime rates among blacks has now been twisted into proof that the system is racist.

> *"Far too many children with unmet mental health needs are ending up in our juvenile justice system—out of luck and behind bars."*

Mentally Ill Youth Should Not Be Placed in the Juvenile Justice System

Tammy Seltzer

Instead of receiving mental health treatment, thousands of mentally ill children are inappropriately placed in the juvenile justice system, maintains Tammy Seltzer in the following viewpoint. Seltzer argues that this trend is both harmful to youth and expensive for the state. She recommends that appropriate mental health services be made available in communities across the United States so that mentally ill youth can be treated rather than warehoused. Seltzer is senior staff attorney for the Bazelon Center for Mental Health Law, a national legal advocate for people with mental disabilities.

As you read, consider the following questions:
1. How much longer do juveniles with mental or emotional disorders stay in detention compared to other youth, according to Seltzer?
2. In the author's opinion, what role do schools play in sending children with mental disorders to the juvenile justice system?
3. How will the Keeping Families Together Act help children with mental or emotional disorders, as argued by Seltzer?

Tammy Seltzer, testimony before the U.S. Senate Committee on Government Affairs, Washington, DC, July 7, 2004.

On any given night, nearly 2,000 children and youth—some as young as seven—languish in juvenile detention facilities across the country because they cannot access needed mental health services. As a result, correction staff struggle to serve a population they are ill equipped to handle, and they and children needlessly risk injury—all at unnecessary taxpayer expense.

Until now, public-policy circles have largely ignored the issue. Recently, however, Representative Henry Waxman (D-CA) and Senator Susan Collins (R-ME) commissioned the first national survey of children with mental health needs unnecessarily incarcerated in juvenile detention centers awaiting treatment. Their findings—released today [July 7, 2004]—highlight a tragic and expensive public policy failure.

Survey Findings

Let me take a moment to highlight some of the key findings. Over a six-month period in 2003, nearly 15,000 incarcerated youth—roughly 8% of all children in the centers surveyed—were detained awaiting mental health services in the community, according to the survey. Many have no criminal charges pending, while others were arrested for minor offenses, such as truancy or trespassing, generally traced to their mental health problems. Worse, investigators noted that the survey probably underestimates the scope of the problem.

Investigators found that juveniles with mental or emotional disorders also stay in detention 36% longer—an average 23.4 days, compared to 17.2 days for all detainees. Living in a punitive and traumatic setting—with very poor mental health services or none at all—their mental health worsens over time.

The rate of self-harm and suicide among juveniles with emotional and mental disorders while incarcerated is four times that of youth overall. Although the issue of victimization was not explicitly addressed in the survey, these incarcerated youth may also be more likely to be victims of violence by other detainees because they appear more vulnerable due to their illness.

Correctional officers are often overwhelmed trying to serve a population they have few resources and little training to help. When officers restrain children for fear that they will hurt themselves or assault others, the children are at risk of severe injury, even death. Attention paid to youth with serious mental health needs diverts resources from monitoring the other juveniles in detention centers.

Incarcerating youth who are waiting for mental health services is not only damaging to the youth; it is also wasteful. Investigators found that this failed policy cost taxpayers almost $100 million in 2003 alone.

My testimony today will address the causes of this tragedy, describe the kinds of services and supports necessary to keep children with emotional and behavioral disorders out of the juvenile justice system, and outline steps the federal government can take to make a difference for these children and their families.

Cause of the Crisis: Access to Care

According to detention center administrators, these children they identified for the survey should not be in their facilities and would not be there if appropriate mental health services and supports were available in the community.

Unfortunately, the number of children with mental illnesses who are inappropriately held in short-term detention facilities is just one particularly nasty symptom of a crisis in children's mental health. According to the Surgeon General, about 5–9% of children ages 9 to 17 are affected by a serious emotional disturbance (SED). Yet nearly four out of five American children who could benefit from mental health services do not receive them. The tattered "safety net" for children with mental illnesses drives too many into the juvenile justice system, then leaves them to wait for scarce community mental health services.

Children with mental disorders are funneled into the juvenile justice system through various routes:

- *Lack of access:* In most communities, the public mental health system is open from 9 to 5, when most children are in school, but the police department is open 24 hours a day. The police are the only public employees who have a duty to respond to every call for help; the mental health system offers too few services and the little they do offer are usually not the kind of intensive, individualized care that we know can prevent children from entering the juvenile justice system.

- *Lack of accountability:* Schools are playing a larger role in sending children with mental disorders to the juvenile justice system. Although legally required to provide positive support and other proactive intervention to address behavioral problems stemming from a student's disability, schools instead invoke zero-tolerance policies and call the police to report even minor violations of school rules.
- *Bias toward law enforcement solutions:* The agencies responsible for supporting parents and treating their children pass the buck by instructing parents to call the police when a child needs help. In one case, a mental health crisis line designed to aid parents called the police instead of sending out a crisis team of mental health professionals, even though mental health services would have been a more effective and humane response.
- *Lack of comprehensive insurance for mental health problems*: Desperate parents of a child with a serious emotional or mental disorder often call police when they can no longer handle their child's behavior because their insurance will not cover the mental health services their child needs and the public mental health system offers no help. Parents with no insurance are even less likely to obtain necessary services; parents with Medicaid coverage are not being offered the kinds of services states could provide under that program.
- *Lack of coordination*: The public agencies that serve children (primarily child welfare, education, mental health and juvenile justice) are so uncoordinated that a child can end up with several different mental health diagnoses, with each agency referring the parents to another for services that simply do not exist.

What Children Need to Succeed

While model programs are far too rare, effective alternatives to incarceration do exist. One such program, Wraparound Milwaukee, works closely with parents to provide services tailored to the needs of each child so children can stay out of crisis and out of the juvenile justice system. The program is reducing costs and—more important—keeping kids out of juvenile detention centers.

Treating Youth Like Adults

They're the faces of children: The 17-year-old sniper with the delicate features and sad, boyish look who took part in a deadly shooting spree that terrorized the nation's capital [in 2002]. The chubby-faced 14-year-old with tears streaming down his cheeks after he was sentenced to life in prison [in 1999] for stomping to death a 6-year-old girl when he was only 12.

As their crimes and their youth shocked the country, the cases of Lee Malvo and Lionel Tate also renewed a debate that for many years has been largely one-sided: how to understand and address the crimes of children. For the past 20 years, the American criminal justice system has dealt with juvenile offenders in a way it never did before: by treating them like adults who are responsible for their actions and must be isolated and punished for their crimes.

The results of that policy, says a growing chorus of psychologists, lawyers, and researchers, is record numbers of young people who are sentenced to juvenile detention facilities that have become warehouses for mentally disturbed youth. "Put bluntly, the juvenile-justice system has become the dumping ground for poor, minority youth with mental disorders and learning disabilities," said Laurence Steinberg, a juvenile-justice researcher and professor of psychology at Temple University.

Rob Waters, *Psychotherapy Networker*, March/April 2004.

Wraparound Milwaukee blends funding from the city's child welfare and juvenile justice agencies and pools it with private and public insurance funds to pay for a coordinated service-delivery system. In its first five years, the program reduced the average monthly cost of care per child from more than $5,000 to less than $3,300. Because the savings were reinvested in the program, Wraparound Milwaukee has been able to nearly double the number of children served. Most important, children's ability to function at home, in school and in the community has improved significantly, and the number returning to the juvenile justice system has been cut in half. In addition, Wraparound Milwaukee has been able to return more than 80% of the children in residential treatment centers to their homes or their communities once the children and their families receive the appropriate individualized, strength-based services.

With such blended funding and cross-agency collaboration, other cities and states could improve access to children's mental health services and reduce the number of children who are needlessly and cruelly detained in juvenile facilities.

Fortunately, we know the principles that make programs like Wraparound Milwaukee successful in helping children avoid juvenile detention and succeed in their communities. Children and their families must have ready access to mental health services and supports, and this access must be based on "kid time," not bankers' hours. Services and supports must be designed to enable children to succeed at home and school, not just avoid detention. Child-serving agencies must be held accountable for serving children well and not rewarded for pushing them off of the agency rolls and into the juvenile justice budget. In particular, schools must be responsible for educating and supporting all of their students; communities must not allow schools to shirk their duties by suspending, expelling and calling the police on students whose behavior could be effectively addressed using positive behavioral supports. In addition, states and the federal government need to do more to end insurance discrimination and to serve the uninsured. . . .

Recommendations for Federal Agencies

Department of Justice
According to today's report, in April 2003 the General Accounting Office [GAO] recommended that the Department of Justice "track the inappropriate detention of mentally ill youth across the country." The Department of Justice declined to follow the GAO's recommendation, citing a lack of information about the problem.

The scope of the problem has now been documented by the Waxman/Collins report, and the evidence shows that the problem is widespread, occurring in two thirds of the surveyed facilities and endangering thousands of children with mental or emotional disorders. Courts have found illegal the practice of holding people in detention facilities solely because mental health services are not available. Given the seriousness of the situation, we urge lawmakers to require the Department of Justice to reconsider the GAO's request and also encourage the department to enforce the law.

Center for Medicare and Medicaid Services

But simply closing the door to juvenile justice is not a panacea. For example, the report notes that many children are in juvenile justice limbo because of a lack of specialized foster care homes. Obviously, children should be kept at home whenever possible, and necessary services should be brought to them there. However, when out-of-home treatment is absolutely necessary, therapeutic foster care has proven effectiveness. In therapeutic foster care, a child is placed with specially trained foster parents and provided intensive, individualized mental health services. In addition to helping the child, therapeutic foster care programs also prepare and support the child's family to enable a successful transition after the child leaves the therapeutic placement. This method is less expensive and less restrictive than other types of out-of-home placement, and studies of children in therapeutic foster care show behavioral improvements and more successful transitions to less restrictive environments.

States can use Medicaid to help pay for some of the costs of therapeutic foster care, but far too few states take advantage of this option due to confusion about what Medicaid covers. The Center for Medicare and Medicaid Services (CMS) could clear up these misunderstandings by issuing a clarifying memo to state Medicaid directors, thus making more funds available for states to expand the number of therapeutic foster care placements they offer.

Department of Education

In 1997, the Individuals with Disabilities Education Act (IDEA) was amended to include specific language about schools' responsibility to respond proactively to students' behavior if it interferes with their learning or the learning of others. The reauthorization explicitly calls for the use of positive behavioral supports and interventions. Research has shown that positive behavioral supports are the most effective way of managing disruptive behavior for all students, not just those with disabilities. One middle school with 550 students saw a 54-percent reduction of office discipline referrals; 300 fights per year dropped to a handful.

Too few schools have embraced positive behavioral supports, relying instead on zero tolerance policies, suspension, expulsion and calling the police—tactics that do nothing to improve student behavior, according to experts in the field. In fact, such strategies increase the likelihood that children will end up in the juvenile justice system. From *Pediatrics* journal:

> *A Centers for Disease Control and Prevention study found that when youth are not in school, they are more likely to become involved in a physical fight and to carry a weapon. Out-of-school adolescents are also more likely to smoke; use alcohol, marijuana, and cocaine; and engage in sexual intercourse. Suicidal ideation and behavior may be expected to occur more often at these times of isolation among susceptible youth.*

The Department of Education must do more to enforce the IDEA for children with emotional and behavioral disorders and to promote the use of school-wide positive behavioral supports for all children.

Recommendations for Congress

Family Opportunity Act

To address the lack of insurance for families of children with severe disabilities, the Senate should also pass the Family Opportunity Act (FOA). The FOA would allow a limited group of families who don't otherwise qualify for Medicaid to be able to buy into the program on a sliding-scale basis for their child, improving access to medically necessary mental health services.[1]

Keeping Families Together Act

The Keeping Families Together Act, introduced last Fall [2003] by Senator Collins and others, would help reduce the number of children with mental or emotional disorders in juvenile detention centers by supporting states' efforts to develop coordinated systems of care.

Treatment for mental health disorders, such as bipolar disorder, depression, schizophrenia and other serious mental ill-

---

1. As of this writing, the FOA and the Keeping Families Together Act had passed the Senate, but had not yet passed the House of Representatives.

nesses can be very expensive. Many parents exhaust their private insurance after just a few months and are ineligible for Medicaid or other assistance due to income and assets. This leaves the parents of a child with a severe mental illness with the agonizing decision between care or custody. No parent should be put in the position of making this decision, and no child belongs in the child welfare or juvenile justice system for the sole purpose of obtaining mental health services.

The Keeping Families Together Act will provide states with the ability to build new infrastructure to more efficiently serve children needing mental health services while keeping them with their families in their own homes. This legislation:

- Provides $55 million over six years in Family Support Grants to states that have committed to providing appropriate mental health services to children so that parents do not have to relinquish custody of their children to get them the help they need. Eligible children and youth are those under age 21 who are in the custody of the state or are at risk of entering care to receive mental health services. Family support services are individualized with family input, provided to the eligible child or youth and their family, and created to promote the mental health of an eligible child or youth;

- Requires collaboration between both private and public partners, including representatives of families of seriously emotionally disturbed children, mental health care providers, private health insurers, hospitals and residential care facilities, as well as state partners, such as the child welfare and juvenile justice agencies among many; and

- Establishes a Federal Interagency Task Force to make recommendations to Congress concerning strategies to improve the delivery of mental health services. The Task Force will work with mental health and child advocates, as well as representatives of affected families and state systems of care, to submit a biannual report to Congress on its progress in implementing recommendations, ending relinquishments and improving the delivery of mental health services.

Policymakers should act soon to adopt these reforms. Far too many children with unmet mental health needs are ending up in our juvenile justice system—out of luck and behind bars.

Immediate Change Is Needed

When I last appeared before this [Senate] committee to discuss the plight of parents having to relinquish custody of their children in order to obtain mental health services, I discussed a GAO study that attempted to document the scope of the problem. The most shocking information in the report was not the number of children who had been torn from their families—the 12,700 figure was most definitely an underestimate of the problem. As someone who has worked exclusively in mental health for eight years, I was most troubled about where these children were ending up. I had assumed that the custody relinquishment problem was a child welfare issue. To my surprise, however, two-thirds of the children were being dumped into the juvenile justice system, while only a third were in child welfare.

Rep. Waxman and Sen. Collins must be commended for requesting this juvenile justice report, which I view as an important follow-up to the GAO study on custody relinquishment. The report is yet another indictment of America's failing mental health system. By providing insufficient support to families in crisis and actively involving the police, the public mental health system criminalizes rather than treats mental health problems in children and youth.

We must demand an immediate change in philosophy and expectations. All child-serving agencies must stop using the juvenile justice system to avoid serving children they don't want, and police and judges should refuse to participate in the criminalization of a public health problem. These children languishing in juvenile detention facilities may have been thrown away like yesterday's garbage, but they will be tomorrow's adults. If we do not take responsibility for meeting their mental health needs now, we are undermining their ability to reach their full potential later, and that would be the greatest tragedy of all.

> *"[The juvenile justice system] has failed to develop programs shaped by girls' unique situations or to address the special problems girls have in a sexist society."*

The Juvenile Justice System Must Address the Needs of Girls

Meda Chesney-Lind

In the following viewpoint Meda Chesney-Lind argues that since the late 1980s girls have been more frequently arrested for criminal behavior and thus make up an increasing percentage of those in the juvenile justice system. However, she points out, the system has not kept up with this change, still tailoring its treatment programs toward boys. She believes that juvenile justice professionals need to begin creating programs that effectively address the unique needs of girls. Chesney-Lind is a professor in the Women's Studies Program at the University of Hawaii at Manoa.

As you read, consider the following questions:
1. In the author's opinion, why is girls' aggression less likely to be reported to authorities?
2. According to Chesney-Lind, what are the most common types of offenses for which girls are arrested?
3. Why do juvenile justice professionals typically prefer working with boys, according to the author?

Meda Chesney-Lind, "Are Girls Closing the Gender Gap in Violence?" *Criminal Justice Magazine*, vol. 16, Spring 2001. Copyright © 2001 by the American Bar Association. All rights reserved. Reproduced by permission.

G irls in the juvenile justice system were once dubbed the "forgotten few." That concept has rapidly faded as the increase in the number of girls arrested has dramatically outstripped that of boys for most of the last decade. Girls now [in 2001] account for one out of four arrests, and statistics show the greatest increase in arrests is for violent offenses. This shift highlights both the need to better understand the dynamics of female delinquency and the need to tailor the criminal justice system's response.

Changes in Arrests

Between 1989 and 1998, arrests of girls increased 50.3 percent, compared to only 16.5 percent for boys, according to the FBI's 1999 report, *Crime in the United States 1998*. During that same period, arrests of girls for serious violent offenses increased by 64.3 percent and arrests of girls for "other assaults" increased an astonishing 125.4 percent. In 1999, the Office of Juvenile Justice and Delinquency Prevention reported that the female violent crime rate for 1997 was 103 percent above the 1981 rate, compared to a 27 percent increase for males, prompting the statement that "increasing juvenile female arrests and the involvement of girls in at-risk and delinquent behavior has been a pervasive trend across the United States." Concomitant with the rising number of arrests are increases in girls' referral to juvenile courts. Between 1988 and 1997, the number of delinquency cases involving girls increased by 83 percent compared to a 39 percent increase for males.

Aggression and Violence

This apparent spike in what might be called girls' "nontraditional" delinquency has to be understood in context: Girls' capacity for aggression and violence has historically been ignored, trivialized, or denied. Perhaps because of this, self-report data, particularly from the 1970s and 1980s, have always shown higher involvement of girls in aggressive behavior than is reflected in official statistics. For example, in a 1976 survey, adolescents reporting on their own behavior showed a male to female ratio of 3.5:1 for serious assault, and a ratio of 3.4:1 for minor assault. Meanwhile, the FBI's 1980 arrest statistics showed a much greater male to female ratio of participation in aggravated assault—5.6:1. Another study reported the ratio of male to female for simple assault at 3.8:1. FBI 1999 arrest statistics show a 3.54:1 ratio for "aggravated assault" and a 2.25:1 ratio for "other assaults." Taken together, these numbers suggest that what we're seeing is not an increase in violence among girls so much as a closing of the gap between what girls have always done (and self-reported) and arrest statistics. . . .

Those who study aggression in children and young adults also note that girls' aggression is usually within the home or "intrafemale" and, thus, likely to be less often reported to authorities. The fact that these forms of aggression have been largely ignored by scholars as well as the general public also means that there is substantial room for girls' aggression to be "discovered" at a time where concern about youth violence is heightened. . . .

Relabeling Status Offenses

What about dramatic increases in arrests of girls for "other assaults"? It cannot be ruled out that relabeling as violent what were once called status offenses—"running away" or "requires supervision"—has had an impact on reported crime rates as has the change in police practices towards domestic violence. A review of more than 2,000 cases of girls referred to Maryland's juvenile justice system for "person-to-person" offenses revealed that virtually all (97.9 percent) involved assault. A closer examination of the records revealed that about half were family centered and involved such activities as a girl hitting her mother and her mother subsequently pressing charges.

More recently, [researcher] Leslie Acoca's study of nearly 1,000 girls' files from four California counties found that while a high percentage of these girls were charged with "person offenses," a majority of these involved assault. Further, "a close reading of the case files of girls charged with assault revealed that most of these charges were the result of nonserious, mutual combat situations with parents." Acoca details cases that she regards as typical, including: "father lunged at her while she was calling the police about a domestic dispute. She (girl) hit him." Finally, she reports that some cases were quite trivial in nature, including a girl arrested "for throwing cookies at her mother."

In essence, when exploring the dramatic increases in the arrests of girls for "other assault," it is likely that changes in enforcement practices have dramatically narrowed the gender gap, including an increase in arrests for domestic violence. A recent California study found that the female share of these arrests increased from 6 percent in 1988 to 16.5 percent in 1998. African-American females had arrest rates roughly three times that of white females.

Relabeling girls' arguments with parents from status offenses to assault is a form of "bootstrapping." It facilitates the incarceration of girls, especially African-Americans, in detention facilities and training schools—something that would not be possible if the girls were arrested for a noncriminal status offense.

Arrests of juveniles for minor or "other" assaults can range from schoolyard tussles to relatively serious assaults. Researchers have noted that an increasing number of arrests of girls for "other assaults" are relatively nonserious in nature and tend to consist of being bystanders or companions to males involved in skirmishes and fights. Often simple assaults without injury are attempted or threatened or not completed. At a time when official concern about youth violence is almost unparalleled and school principals are increasingly likely to call police to their campuses, it should come as no surprise that youthful arrests in this area are up. . . .

Nonaggressive Offenses and Drug Use

Examining the types of offenses for which girls are arrested, it is clear that most are arrested for the less serious criminal acts and status offenses (noncriminal juvenile offenses such as running away or curfew violation). In 1998, roughly half of the arrests of girls were for either larceny theft, mostly shoplifting (21.5 percent), or status offenses (22.1 percent.)

Status offenses have always played a significant role in bringing girls into contact with the criminal justice system. They accounted for about a quarter of all arrests of girls in 1998, but only 10 percent of arrests of boys—figures that remained relatively stable during the last decade. In 1998, more than half of those arrested for running away from home were girls. Running away and prostitution remain the only two categories where more girls than boys are arrested. Arrest rates for these activities have remained stable or climbed in recent years, despite passage of the Juvenile Justice and Delinquency Prevention Act in 1974, which encouraged state and local jurisdictions to divert and deinstitutionalize young people charged with status offenses. Between 1989 and 1998, according to 1999 FBI statistics, the number of girls arrested nationally for running away remained about the same, but arrests of girls for curfew violations increased by an astonishing 238.5 percent.

A Male Norm in Sentencing

The circumstances surrounding the commission of a crime vary significantly between men and women. Yet penalties are most often based on the circumstances of crimes committed by men, creating a male norm in sentencing, which makes the much-touted gender neutrality of guideline sentencing very problematical. In those circumstances when the pattern of conduct involved in women's commission of a crime is ignored or almost totally subordinated to the male pattern, it becomes all the more important to consider the variants that characterize women's commission of the crime in meting out individual sentences. This, in my opinion, is at the heart of the Federal Sentencing Guidelines' gender bias. While commanding that gender never be a relevant factor in sentencing, the Guidelines nonetheless base their core sentences on a predominantly male behavior pattern.

Patricia M. Wald, *Criminal Justice Magazine*, Spring 2001.

Why are girls more likely to be arrested than boys for running away from home? There are no simple answers. Studies of delinquency—not simply arrests—show that girls and boys run away from home in about equal numbers. [Researcher] Rachelle J. Canter found in a national youth survey that there was no evidence of greater female involvement in any category of delinquent behavior. Indeed, in this sample, males were significantly more likely than females to self-report status offenses. There is some evidence to suggest that parents and police may respond differently to the same behavior. Parents may call the police more frequently when their daughters do not come home, and police may be more likely to arrest a female than a male runaway. . . .

Sexual and Physical Abuse

Research shows that boys and girls often have different reasons for running away. Girls are much more likely to be victims of childhood sexual abuse—some experts estimate that roughly 70 percent of the victims of child sexual abuse are girls. Not surprisingly, the evidence also suggests a link between this problem and female delinquency—particularly running away from home.

Studies of girls on the streets and in court populations show high rates of both sexual and physical abuse. A study of a runaway shelter in Toronto found that 73 percent of girls and 38 percent of boys had been sexually abused. The same study found that sexually abused female runaways were more likely than their nonabused counterparts to engage in criminal activities such as theft and prostitution. No such pattern was found in abused boys.

Detailed research on young people entering the juvenile justice system in Florida has compared the constellations of problems presented by girls and boys entering detention. These studies found that female adolescents were more likely to have abuse histories and contact with the juvenile justice system for status offenses, while male youth had higher rates of involvement with various delinquent offenses. Further research on a larger group admitted to an assessment center in Tampa concluded that "girls' problem behavior commonly relates to an abusive and traumatizing home life, whereas boys' law violating behavior reflects their involvement in a delinquent lifestyle."

More recent research confirms these observations. In a study of the backgrounds of 96 girls in the custody of the California Youth Authority, researchers compared these results with those garnered from a comparison sample of male youth. They found that boys were more likely to be traumatized as observers of violence, but "girls were more likely to be traumatized as direct victims." As a result, it's possible that girls are more likely than boys to suffer post–traumatic stress disorder; the levels of the disorder found in the re-searched population were "significantly higher than among the general adolescent female population"—65 percent compared to 11 percent. About two-thirds of the girls were serving time for a violent offense (murder, assault, and rob-bery) and 43 percent were identified as gang members.

Program as If Girls Matter

National data indicate that between 1988 and 1997 deten-tions involving girls increased by 65 percent compared to a 30 percent increase for boys. San Francisco researchers ex-amined the situation of girls in their juvenile justice system and concluded they frequently languished in detention cen-ters waiting for placement, while the boys were released or put in placement. As a result, 60 percent of the girls were de-tained for more than seven days, compared to only 6 percent of the boys. These figures reflect a system that has failed to develop programs shaped by girls' unique situations or to address the special problems girls have in a sexist society.

Part of the challenge is that girls remain all but invisible in programs for youth and in the literature available to those who work with youth. For example, a 1993 study of the San Francisco Chapter of the National Organization for Women found that only 8.7 percent of the programs funded by the major city organization funding children and youth pro-grams "specifically addressed the needs of girls." Not sur-prisingly, then, a 1995 study of youth participation in San Francisco afterschool or summer sports programs found only 26 percent of the participants were girls.

In addition, people who work in the juvenile justice system typically prefer working with boys and routinely stress the "difficulty" of working with girls. According to one study, ju-venile justice professionals who work with both male and fe-male adolescents talk almost exclusively about their male clients. Likewise, in 1997, [researcher] Christine Alder noted that "willful" girls produce problems for a system devised to handle boys: professionals in these systems often conceptual-ize girls as "hysterical," "manipulative," "verbally aggressive," and "untrusting" while boys are "honest," "open," and "less complex." Clearly, the juvenile justice system has its work cut out for it if it hopes to deal fairly with girls, to say nothing of creating programs and services tailored to girls' problems and needs.

Alder also notes that serving girls effectively will require different and innovative strategies since young men tend to be more noticeable and noticed than young women. When girls go out, they tend to move in smaller groups, they face greater proscriptions against "hanging out," and they may justifiably fear being on the streets at night. Finally, girls have many more domestic expectations than do boys, and these may keep them confined to their homes. Alder notes that this may be a particular issue for immigrant girls.

Given what we know about girls' problems, including girls' aggression and violence, what should effective programs for troubled girls look like? They should address the following:

- dealing with the physical and sexual violence in their lives (from parents, boyfriends, pimps, and others);
- confronting the risk of HIV/AIDS;
- handling pregnancy and motherhood;
- coping with drug and alcohol dependency, facing family problems;
- dealing with employment training and unemployment;
- finding safe housing;
- managing stress; and
- developing a sense of efficacy and empowerment.

Many of these needs are universal and should be part of programs for all youth. However, most are particularly important for young women. Juvenile justice professionals should also scrutinize programs to ensure that they are culturally-specific as well as gender-specific. Since girls of color experience their gender differently than do their white counterparts, programs to divert and deinstitutionalize must respond to the unique developmental issues confronting minority girls. They must also build in the specific cultural resources available in ethnic communities.

Programs, particularly those that are issue-specific, also need to provide transition and after-care services that support the progress young women make. Girls' programs also need to create separate time and space for girls, apart from boys, so that concerns about sexism will not be overshadowed by boys' more disruptive behavior. Programs, particularly prevention programs for girls, need to begin at earlier ages. Many at-risk girls may engage in delinquent behavior simply because there is little else to occupy their free time. Structured recreation that gets past the girls-watching-boys-play-sports approach should be vigorously explored. Girls in the juvenile justice system often say that they probably would have avoided arrest had they had opportunities to engage in meaningful, interesting activities.

Finally, programs should work to empower girls and advocate for change that will benefit girls. This entails not only building on girls' innate strengths, skills, and creativity to develop their voices and their abilities to assert themselves, but also identifying and challenging barriers that girls, particularly marginalized girls, face in our society.

| *"Not only can privatization lead to abuses
but it doesn't even necessarily save money."*

Privatization Within the Juvenile Justice System Must Be Stopped

Eyal Press and Jennifer Washburn

Attempts to privatize juvenile corrections facilities in the United States have been harmful to youth, argue Eyal Press and Jennifer Washburn in the following viewpoint. According to the authors, privatization has failed because it is impossible to provide quality care for juveniles and make a profit at the same time. Indeed, private companies running prisons and treatment centers focus on profits rather than treatment, which has led to the abuse of young criminals, Press and Washburn maintain. Press is a freelance writer and Washburn is a fellow at the New America Foundation.

As you read, consider the following questions:

1. What did the SunTrust report reveal about privatization opportunities, according to the authors?
2. Why are large facilities often harmful for kids, as argued by Barry Krisberg?
3. What has made it especially difficult to monitor youth services, according to the authors?

In August of 2000 the National Center for Children in Poverty, at Columbia University, released a study showing that despite the country's recent economic boom, 13 million American children were living in poverty—three million more than in 1979. For most Americans that was unsettling news, but for a small group of publicly traded companies it represented an opportunity. As the ranks of children living in poverty have grown during the past two decades, so have the ranks of juveniles filing through the nation's dependency and deliquency courts, typically landing in special-education programs, psychiatric-treatment centers, orphanages, and juvenile prisons. These were formerly run almost exclusively by non-profit and public agencies. In the mid-1990s, however, a number of large, multi-state for-profit companies emerged to form what Wall Street soon termed the "at-risk-youth industry."

Compelling Incentives

The financial incentives were compelling. In 1997 SunTrust Equitable Securities, one of the nation's leading investment firms, published a forty-five-page report titled "At-Risk Youth . . . A Growth Industry" which estimated that annual public spending on youth services amounted to $50 billion. The report appeared shortly after Congress passed the 1996 Welfare Reform Act, which included a provision allowing for-profit companies to tap into child-welfare funds that had previously been reserved largely for nonprofit agencies.

The SunTrust report documented an array of disquieting social trends—including rising numbers of children living with single parents and in working-poor families—that from the industry's perspective sounded like good news. "Not only has the raw number of abused and neglected children increased," SunTrust observed, "but . . . the rate of children reported as abused and neglected has increased from 28 per 1,000 children in 1984 to 43 per 1,000 in 1993." A diagram titled the "Privatization Spectrum" showed how companies could profit as children cycled "from the schoolhouse to the jailhouse," passing through one publicly funded, privately run facility after another. Arrows marked the flow of kids to companies offering programs in special education (a $32 billion market), child welfare ($12–$15 billion), and juvenile justice ($3.5 billion). No arrows indicated how these children might one day exit the system and lead ordinary lives.

Privatization Failures

Today [2002], five years after the release of the SunTrust report, the prospects for the at-risk-youth industry are less rosy. Claims that contracting out social services would improve efficiency and lower costs have not panned out—and the projected windfalls for private contractors have failed to materialize. Many state and local governments, however, continue to entrust social services to profit-driven companies. Examining the records of some of the industry's leaders highlights the substantial social costs of doing so.

Consider the Pahokee Youth Development Center, a 350-bed facility for "moderate-risk" youth, set on the northern edge of the Everglades [Florida] and opened, in 1997, by Correctional Services Corporation [CSC], one of the nation's largest at-risk-youth companies. James Slattery, CSC's co-founder and CEO [chief executive officer], promised that the facility would save taxpayers money while turning out "reformed, treated youths." But in 1998 an independent monitor assigned by the state found inadequate staff training and insufficient medical services, and the Florida Department of Juvenile Justice's inspector general confirmed numerous cases in which staff members had used "unnecessary and improper force" against youths.

CSC—which denied requests for interviews—seemed more interested in finding creative ways to maximize revenue than in rehabilitating kids. Although the state paid the company some $2.5 million a year to provide education, Pahokee failed to maintain proper student records, and for several weeks in the 1998 school year it held no classes whatsoever. A company document has revealed that CSC intentionally delayed the release of ten juveniles so as to maintain the head count, which determined payment. The following year, after Pahokee failed its second state quality-assurance review, CSC canceled its contract, and the facility was taken over by another company. . . .

To be sure, problems in the youth-services field are by no means confined to the private sector. In both the mental-

Public Versus Private Management of Juvenile Facilities in Florida

	State-operated	For-profit	Non-profit	County-operated
Number of Facilities	31	20	107	11
Clients Released	1,827	1,115	4,825	633
% Recidivate in First Year	49.1%	55.9%	47.0%	48.5%
Mean Felonies per Individual	4.24	6.19	4.40	6.00
Mean Cost ($) per Release	16,253	20,912	18,703	22,984
Mean Stay (Days) for All Clients	134	211	161	202
Mean Age Exit for All Clients	15.65	15.89	15.57	16.10
Mean Facility Size	25.1	143.7	20.3	83.3

Patrick Bayer and David E. Pozen, Economic Growth Center, Yale University, July 2003.

health and juvenile-justice fields, in fact, it was government's failure to provide adequate care that paved the way for privatization: a series of class-action lawsuits in the 1970s and 1980s forced states to shut down many abusive government-run mental-health institutions, and the 1974 Juvenile Justice and Delinquency Prevention Act provided states with federal funding to develop community-based treatment services as an alternative to incarceration with adults. A small contracting empire arose in response, with millions of dollars available to private providers of services. During this first wave of privatization, contracts were awarded mostly to nonprofit and mom-and-pop organizations, many of which pioneered small, local programs in which staff members could develop close relationships with youths. Not until the 1990s did large, multi-state, for-profit companies—some, such as Wackenhut and Correctional Corporation of America, having earlier cut their teeth in the adult prison industry—become major players in the bidding process. They were enticed, in part, by the per diems attached to juveniles, which are higher than those for adults. (Juveniles are eligible for rehabilitative services such as education and mental health.)

Focusing on Capacity

When assesssing the strength of these companies, Wall Street analysts have focused not on treatment methods or philosophy but on capacity. Investment reports highlight each company's recent acquisitions, referred to as "wins," and tally up the number of new "beds/slots." Although some companies do run a variety of smaller programs, industry leaders admit to a preference for large facilities. "I look at it in terms of size," Luis Lamela says. "What we look for is the achievement of economies of scale."

The trouble is that large-scale institutions rarely offer individualized treatment. According to Barry Krisberg, the president of the National Council on Crime and Delinquency [NCCD], a substantial body of evidence shows that smaller programs are more conducive to rehabilitation. One NCCD study found that youths from Massachusetts, a state that runs mostly small-scale programs, had lower rates of recidivism than youths from California, which relies heavily on large institutions. In 2000 an array of leading advocacy groups, including the National Urban League and the American Youth Policy Forum, issued a report calling for a shift in resources away from large-scale, prisonlike facilities and toward community-based, early-stage treatment and prevention programs. "Along with large facilities comes too few staff for too many kids," Krisberg says. "Administrators start to resort to stringent security measures—shakedowns, lockdowns—and the facility starts to look and feel like a prison. . . . There's a replication of the conflicts in the streets."

Abuses and Financial Losses

Not only can privatization lead to abuses but it doesn't even necessarily save money. In Alabama, for example, after a 1993 federal court order required that the state improve rehabilitative services for juvenile delinquents, the Department of Youth Services quickly turned to the private sector. Among the companies that won contracts were Ramsay, CCS, and an Alabama-based company named Three Springs. Henry Mabry, the state's finance director at the time, told us that he first grew suspicious in 1999, when the DYS [Department of Youth Services], whose budget nearly tripled from 1993 to 1998, approached him with a request for $24 million in supplemental funding over the next two years. Shocked at the amount of the request, Mabry examined the contracts and discovered not only that empty beds were available in less costly, state-run facilities but also that there were huge disparities in funding rates: some providers, including CCS, were being paid as much as $142 a day per child, whereas others received less than $70.

Almost every private contract issued by Alabama's Department of Youth Services from 1994 to 1998 was awarded without any request for proposals or competitive bids; state records show that Ramsay, CCS, and Three Springs were all clients of the Bloom Group, a powerful Montgomery lobbying firm. And James Dupree, who had been the director of the DYS during the peak period of privatization, became a lobbyist for Bloom shortly after leaving public office, in September of 1998. . . .

Such problems arise in state after state. As Elliott Star, a professor of urban planning at Columbia [University, New York], points out in his book *You Don't Always Get What You Pay For: The Economics of Privatization*, states often fail to conduct internal cost assessments to determine what private contractors should be paid, even though there is clear evidence that companies frequently tailor their bids to accord with such assessments. Many states also invest inadequately in monitoring.

Monitoring youth services has become especially challenging in recent years, because in the mid-1990s government agencies began shipping juveniles across state lines. In 1999 Florence Simcoe, a former clinical director at Century HealthCare, which operated treatment centers for mentally disturbed children in Phoenix, told the *Chicago Tribune* that she marketed her company's services to officials in Illinois. At-risk children, she said, were "bodies that we got $300 a day for." Barry Krisberg highlights the problem. "We have less regulation of the interstate commerce in troubled kids than of meat products," he says. . . .

Five years ago Wall Street had almost limitless hopes for the at-risk-youth industry, but times have changed. Although all but one of the at-risk-youth companies we spoke with in our initial research are still in operation (the exception is CCS, which was bought out in January of 2002 and is now part of Keys Group Holding), their profits have stagnated, their stock prices have fallen, and current prospects for growth are uncertain. The problem, according to Bob Weaver, is a basic one: "There just isn't enough money in serving these kids to deliver quality and still turn a profit."

Periodical Bibliography

The following articles have been selected to supplement the diverse views presented in this chapter.

Fox Butterfield "Racial Disparities Seen as Pervasive in Juvenile Justice," *New York Times*, April 26, 2000.

Angie Cannon "Juvenile Injustice," *U.S. News & World Report*, August 9, 2004.

E. Michael Foster, Amir Qaseem, and Tim Connor "Can Better Mental Health Services Reduce the Risk of Juvenile Justice System Involvement?" *American Journal of Public Health*, May 2004.

Annette Fuentes "Unchained: From the Bay Area to the Big Apple, Youth Activists Target Juvenile Jails," *In These Times*, July 8, 2002.

Arthur Jones "Juvenile Justice: Speakers at California Parish Strip Away Illusions of Fairness of the U.S. System," *National Catholic Reporter*, April 23, 2004.

Susan McClelland "Institutional Correction: A New Youth Crime Act Aims to Fix a Broken System," *Maclean's*, June 9, 2003.

Angela Neustatter "Prison Can Be the Right Place for Kids," *New Statesman*, August 19, 2002.

Matt Olson "Kids in the Hole," *Progressive*, August 2003.

Ann Patchett "The Age of Innocence," *New York Times Magazine*, September 29, 2002.

Hugh B. Price "America's System of Juvenile Injustice," *San Diego Union-Tribune*, May 3, 2000.

Sarah Sandra and Katz Simkins "Criminalizing Abused Girls," *Violence Against Women*, December 2002.

Zelda D.T. Soriano "Girls in a Playground Called Prison: They Are Little Girls, Mostly Poor, Who Ran Afoul of the Law. What Is the Government Doing to Help Them?" *Women in Action*, December 2003.

Rob Waters "Adult Time for Adult Crime: Have We Lost Faith in Rehabilitating Juvenile Offenders?" *Psychotherapy Networker*, March/April 2004.

For Further Discussion

Chapter 1

1. Joe Lieberman and Jeff McIntyre maintain that the media contribute to youth violence. Henry Jenkins contends that violent youth seek out violent media content. After reading these two viewpoints, do you think that the media is responsible for causing juvenile violence and crime? Why or why not?

2. Sanford Newman and his colleagues make the argument that poor child care increases the chance that children will become juvenile criminals. According to J.E. Keeler, however, juvenile crime can occur despite good parenting. Which author uses the most convincing evidence to support his or her argument? Which evidence is the least convincing? Back up your answers with examples from the texts.

3. Richard Matthews, Daniel G. Jennings, and Bill Dedman present three different arguments about the causes of school violence. After reading their assertions, what do you believe causes school violence? Do you think there is one major risk factor, a combination of factors, or none at all? Explain your answers, citing from the texts.

Chapter 2

1. Don Boys and Daniel L. Myers argue that youth who commit violent crimes need to be held accountable for their actions and should be punished severely. Steven A. Drizin, Stephen K. Harper, and Malcom C. Young maintain, however, that juvenile criminals do not have the same moral understanding as adults do, and thus should not be treated the same as adult criminals. Do you think juvenile criminals should be treated the same way as adult criminals? Explain your answer, citing from the texts.

2. According to J. Steven Smith, incarcerating juveniles with adults is both ineffective and harmful. In contrast, James C. Backstrom claims that juveniles can be effectively and safely housed in adult facilities. What are the advantages of imprisoning juveniles in the same facilities as adults? Do you think there are any disadvantages that might outweigh the advantages? Explain.

3. Malcom C. Young argues that juveniles do not fare well in adult courts. He believes they should remain in juvenile court where they receive age-appropriate treatment. What examples does Young use to support his thesis? Which do you find the most convincing? Which do you find the least convincing?

Chapter 3

1. Kenneth W. Sukhia, Laura H. Carnell, Steve Christian, and James A. Gondles Jr. present different arguments about the best way to prevent juvenile crime. After reading their viewpoints, what do you think is the most effective way to deter youth from committing crimes? Do you think only one prevention strategy should be used, or would a combination of methods be most effective? Explain.

2. Kenneth W. Sukhia maintains that failure to harshly punish juvenile offenders leads to more crime while Laura H. Carnell argues that harsh punishments may actually increase the incidence of juvenile crime. In your opinion, is harsh punishment an effective deterrent of juvenile crime? Back up your answer with examples from the texts.

3. John R. Lott Jr. argues that teachers should be armed to prevent school violence. Jacquelyn Mitchard contends that arming teachers will actually make children less safe. List the support that each author uses to back up his or her contention. In your opinion, which author makes the strongest case about arming teachers? Why?

Chapter 4

1. Eileen Poe-Yamagata and Michael A. Jones argue that the juvenile justice system treats minority youth more harshly than white youth. Jared Taylor contends that juvenile whites and minorities are treated equally. Based on their arguments, do you believe discrimination against minorities is a serious problem in the juvenile justice system? Support your answer.

2. Tammy Seltzer and Meda Chesney-Lind make different arguments about what is wrong with the U.S. juvenile justice system. After reading these two viewpoints, what do you think is the most serious problem with the way that juvenile criminals are treated in the United States? Use statistics and examples from the texts to support your answer.

3. What arguments, examples, and statistics does Tammy Seltzer use to support her contention that mentally ill youth should not be placed in the juvenile justice system? Rank her arguments from most convincing to least convincing.

Organizations to Contact

The editors have compiled the following list of organizations concerned with the issues debated in this book. The descriptions are derived from materials provided by the organizations. All have publications or information available for interested readers. The list was compiled on the date of publication of the present volume; names, addresses, phone and fax numbers, and e-mail addresses may change. Be aware that many organizations take several weeks or longer to respond to inquiries, so allow as much time as possible.

ABA Juvenile Justice Center
740 Fifteenth St. NW, Washington, DC 20005
(202) 662-1506 • fax: (202) 662-1501
e-mail: juvjus@abanet.org • Web site: www.abanet.org

An organization of the American Bar Association, the Juvenile Justice Center disseminates information on juvenile justice systems across the country. The center provides leadership to state and local practitioners, bar associations, judges, youth workers, correctional agency staff, and policy makers. Its publications include the *Juvenile Justice Standards*, a twenty-four volume set of comprehensive juvenile justice standards, and the quarterly *Criminal Justice Magazine*.

American Civil Liberties Union (ACLU)
125 Broad St., New York, NY 10004
(212) 549-2900 • fax: (212) 869-9065
e-mail: aclu@aclu.org • Web site: www.aclu.org

The ACLU is a national organization that works to defend Americans' civil rights as guaranteed by the U.S. Constitution. It opposes curfew laws for juveniles and seeks to protect the public-assembly rights of gang members or people associated with gangs. Among the ACLU's numerous publications are the handbook *The Rights of Prisoners: A Comprehensive Guide to the Legal Rights of Prisoners Under Current Law*, and the briefing paper "Crime and Civil Liberties."

American Correctional Association (ACA)
4380 Forbes Blvd., Lanham, MD 20706
(800) 222-5646 • fax: (301) 918-1886
e-mail: jeffw@aca.org • Web site: www.corrections.com

The ACA is composed of correctional administrators, prison wardens, superintendents, and other corrections professionals who want to improve correctional standards. The association studies the causes of crime and juvenile delinquency and reports regularly on juvenile justice issues in its monthly magazines *Corrections Today* and *Corrections Compendium.*

Center for the Study of Youth Policy
University of Pennsylvania School of Social Work
4200 Pine St., 2nd Fl., Philadelphia, PA 19104
(215) 898-2229 • fax: (215) 573-2791
e-mail: yep@ssw.upenn.edu • Web site: www.kidspolicy.org
The center studies issues concerning juvenile justice and youth corrections. Although it does not take positions regarding these issues, it publishes individuals' opinions in booklets, including *Home-Based Services for Serious and Violent Juvenile Offenders, Youth Violence: An Overview,* and *Mediation Involving Juveniles: Ethical Dilemmas and Policy Questions.*

Committee for Children
2203 Airport Way S., Suite 500, Seattle, WA 98134
(206) 343-1223 • fax: (206) 343-1445
e-mail: info@cfchildren.org • Web site: www.cfchildren.org
The Committee for Children is an international organization that develops classroom curricula and videos as well as teacher, parent, and community training programs for the prevention of child abuse and youth violence. Second Step, the committee's violence prevention curriculum, teaches children social skills and provides training for parents and teachers to practice and reinforce these skills with children. The committee publishes the newsletter *Prevention Update* three times a year and developed the program Second Step, which teaches children to change behaviors and attitudes that contribute to violence.

Educational Fund to End Handgun Violence
Ceasefire Action Network
1000 Sixteenth St. NW, Suite 603, Washington, DC 20036
(202) 530-5888 • fax: (202) 544-7213
e-mail: edfund@aol.com • Web site: www.csgv.org
The fund examines and helps educate the public about handgun violence in the United States and how such violence affects children in particular. It participates in the development of educational materials and programs to help persuade teenagers not to carry guns, and it examines the impact of handguns on public health. The fund's publications include the booklet *Kids and Guns: A National Disgrace* and the quarterly newsletters *Assault Weapon and Accessories in America* and *Firearms Litigation Reporter.*

National Center on Institutions and Alternatives (NCIA)
635 Slaters Ln., Suite G-100, Alexandria, VA 22314
(703) 684-0373 • fax: (703) 684-6073
e-mail: info@ncia.net • Web site: www.igc.org
The NCIA works to reduce the number of people institutionalized in prisons and mental hospitals. It favors the least restrictive forms of detention for juvenile offenders and opposes sentencing juveniles as adults and executing juvenile murderers. The NCIA publishes the report *Youth Homicide: Keeping Perspective on How Many Children Kill* and the article "Justice: Facts vs. Anger."

National Council of Juvenile and Family Court Judges
University of Nevada
1041 N. Virginia St., PO Box 8970, Reno, NV 89557
(775) 784-6012 • fax: (775) 784-6628
e-mail: admin@ncjfcj.org • Web site: www.ncjfcj.org
The council is composed of juvenile and family court judges and other juvenile justice professionals. It seeks to improve family court standards and practices. Its publications include the monthly *Juvenile and Family Law Digest* and the quarterly *Juvenile and Family Court Journal.*

National Council on Crime and Delinquency (NCCD)
685 Market St., Suite 620, San Francisco, CA 94105
(415) 896-6223 • fax: (415) 896-5109
Web site: www.nccd-crc.org
The NCCD is composed of corrections specialists and others interested in the juvenile justice system and the prevention of crime and delinquency. It advocates community-based treatment programs rather than imprisonment for delinquent youth. It opposes placing minors in adult jails and executing those who commit capital offenses before the age of eighteen. The NCCD publishes the quarterlies *Crime and Delinquency* and *Journal of Research in Crime and Delinquency* as well as policy papers, including the "Juvenile Justice Policy Statement."

National Crime Prevention Council (NCPC)
1000 Connecticut Ave. NW, 8th Fl., Washington, DC 20006
(202) 466-6272 • fax: (202) 296-1356
e-mail: webmaster@ncpc.org • Web site: www.ncpc.org
The NCPC provides training and technical assistance to groups and individuals interested in crime prevention. It advocates job training and recreation programs as a means to reduce youth crime and violence. The council, which sponsors the Take a Bite Out of Crime

campaign, is publisher of the book *Changing Perspective: Youth as Resources*, the booklet *Securing the Future for Safer Youth Communities*, and the newsletter *Catalyst*.

National Juvenile Detention Association (NJDA)

Eastern Kentucky University
301 Perkins Building, 521 Lancaster Ave., Richmond, KY 40475
(606) 622-6259 • fax: (606) 622-2333
e-mail: njda@njda.org • Web site: www.njda.org

The NJDA works to advance the science, processes, and art of juvenile detention through overall improvement of the juvenile justice profession. The project's efforts include the delivery of products to juvenile justice and detention facilities, reviewing and establishing detention standards and practices, and stimulating the development of training programs for detention service officials. Its publications include the journal *Developing Comprehensive Systems for Troubled Youth* and the *Journal for Juvenile Justice and Detention Services*.

Office of Juvenile Justice and Delinquency Prevention (OJJDP)

810 Seventh St. NW, Washington, DC 20531
(202) 307-5911 • fax: (202) 307-2093
e-mail: askjj@ojp.usdoj.gov • Web site: ojjdp.ncjrs.gov

As the primary federal agency charged with monitoring and improving the juvenile justice system, the OJJDP develops and funds programs on juvenile justice. Among its goals are the prevention and control of illegal drug use and serious crime by juveniles. Through its Juvenile Justice Clearinghouse, the OJJDP distributes reports such as *Juvenile Offenders in Residential Placement* and *A Comprehensive Guide Response to America's Youth Gang Problem*.

Youth Crime Watch of America

9300 S. Dadeland Blvd., Suite 100, Miami, FL 33156
(305) 670-2409 • fax: (305) 670-3805
e-mail: ycwa@ycwa.org • Web site: www.ycwa.org

Youth Crime Watch of America is dedicated to establishing Youth Crime Watch programs across the United States. It strives to give youth the tools and guidance necessary to actively reduce crime and drug use in schools and communities. Its publications include *Talking to Youth About Crime Prevention* and the workbook *Community Based Youth Crime Watch Program Handbook*.

Bibliography of Books

Susan Abramsky — *Hard Time Blues: How Politics Built a Prison Nation.* New York: St. Martin's, 2002.

Robert Agnew — *Juvenile Delinquency: Causes and Control.* Los Angeles: Roxbury, 2000.

James F. Anderson — *Boot Camps: An Intermediate Sanction.* Lanham, MD: University of America Press, 2000.

Neil I. Bernstein — *How to Keep Your Teenager Out of Trouble and What to Do If You Can't.* New York: Workman, 2001.

Randy Blazak and Wayne S. Wooden — *Renegade Kids, Suburban Outlaws: From Youth Culture to Delinquency.* Florence, KY: Wadsworth, 2000.

Meda Chesney-Lind — *The Female Offender: Girls, Women, and Crime.* Thousand Oaks, CA: Sage, 2004.

Philip J. Cook and Jens Ludwig — *Gun Violence: The Real Costs.* New York: Oxford University Press, 2000.

Gordon A. Crews and Reid H. Montgomery — *Chasing Shadows: Confronting Juvenile Violence in America.* Upper Saddle River, NJ: Prentice-Hall, 2001.

G. David Curry and Scott H. Decker — *Confronting Gangs: Crime and Community.* Los Angeles: Roxbury, 2001.

Scott H. Decker, ed. — *Policing Gangs and Youth Violence.* Belmont, CA: Wadsworth, 2003.

Anthony N. Doob and Carla Cesaroni — *Responding to Youth Crime in Canada.* Toronto: University of Toronto Press, 2004.

Joy G. Dryfoos — *Safe Passage: Making It Through Adolescence in a Risky Society.* New York: Oxford University Press, 2000.

Jeffrey Ferro — *Juvenile Crime.* New York: Facts On File, 2003.

Ronald B. Flowers — *Kids Who Commit Adult Crimes: Serious Criminality by Juvenile Offenders.* New York: Haworth, 2002.

Gustav Mark Gedatus — *Gangs and Violence (Perspectives on Violence).* Santa Rosa, CA: Lifematters, 2000.

Bernard Golden — *Healthy Anger: How to Help Children and Teens Manage Their Anger.* Oxford, UK: Oxford University Press, 2003.

Thomas Grisso and Robert G. Schwartz, eds.	*Youth on Trial: A Developmental Perspective on Juvenile Justice.* Chicago: University of Chicago Press, 2000.
Susan Guarino-Ghezzi	*Balancing Juvenile Justice.* Brunswick, NJ: Transaction, 2004.
Richard Hill and Anthony McMahon	*Families, Crime, and Juvenile Justice.* New York: Peter Lang, 2000.
Thomas A. Jacobs	*Teens on Trial: Twenty Teens Who Challenged the Law—and Changed Your Life.* Minneapolis: Free Spirit, 2000.
Thomas B. Jacobs	*Can Gun Control Work?* New York: Oxford University Press, 2002.
Michael J. Leiber	*The Contexts of Juvenile Justice Decision Making: When Race Matters.* Albany: State University of New York Press, 2003.
José M. López	*Gangs: Casualties in an Undeclared War.* Dubuque, IA: Kendall/Hunt, 2002.
Jens Ludwig and Philip J. Cook, eds.	*Evaluating Gun Policy: Effects on Crime and Violence.* Washington, DC: Brookings Institution, 2003.
Jody Miller	*One of the Guys: Girls, Gangs, and Gender.* New York: Oxford University Press, 2000.
John K. Mooradian	*Disproportionate Confinement of African-American Juvenile Delinquents.* New York: LFB Scholarly, 2003.
Wilda Webber Morris	*Stop the Violence: Educating Ourselves to Protect Our Youth.* Valley Forge, PA: Judson Press, 2001.
David L. Myers	*Excluding Youth from Juvenile Court: The Effectiveness of Legislative Waiver.* New York: LFB Scholarly Publishing, 2001.
John Pitts	*The New Politics of Youth Crime: Discipline and Solidarity.* New York: St. Martin's, 2001.
Henry Ruth and Kevin R. Reitz	*The Challenge of Crime: Rethinking Our Response.* Cambridge, MA: Harvard University Press, 2003.
Josh Sugarman	*Every Handgun Is Aimed at You: The Case for Banning Handguns.* New York: New Press, 2001.
Michael Tonry and Anthony N. Doob, eds.	*Youth Crime and Youth Justice: Comparative and Cross-National Perspectives.* Chicago: University of Chicago Press, 2004.

Joseph G. Weiss, Robert D. Crutchfield, and George S. Bridges	*Juvenile Delinquency: Readings.* Boston: Pine Forge, 2001.
Susan O. White, ed.	*Handbook of Youth and Justice.* New York: Kluwer Academic/Plenum, 2001.
James Q. Wilson and Joan Petersilia	*Crime: Public Policies for Crime Control.* Oakland, CA: ICS, 2002.
Kenneth Wooden and Kathleen M. Heide	*Weeping in the Playtime of Others: America's Incarcerated Children.* Columbus: Ohio State University Press, 2000.

Index

208